CASERTA
Tattoo
Convention
8th Edition

DGN MAGAZINE TATTOO

12·13·14
APRILE
2024

Kush Trece

DGN TATTOO MAG

XIX YEAR - MONTHLY EDITION
NOVEMBER 2023 - #164

DIRECTOR:

Sebastian Harbaruk
eventosdgn@hotmail.com

WEB PRODUCER AND EDITOR

Ibrahin Harbaruk / Lautaro Tinti

DESIGN AND EDITORIAL PRODUCTION OF

De La Madre Producciones
delamadre@gmail.com

PHOTOGRAPHY

Leyla Ferreyra
ph.editorial@dgn.com
Pancha Carolga Harbaruk
pancha@gmail.com

TRANSLATIONS

Flor Antonietti
florantonietti@yahoo.com.ar

ADMINISTRATION

Pablo Di Gruccio
pablodigruccio@gmail.com

MARKETING AND SALES

Estrella Ferreyra
dgntattoomag@hotmail.com
+549 11 30073999
Facebook.com/dgntattoomag

SUBSCRIPTIONS

dgntattoomag@gmail.com

DGN TATTOO MAGAZINE
is a registered trademark

CONTACTS

USA +1 (213) 633-7712
LATAM +54 9 11-3007-3999
eventosdgn@hotmail.com

FOLLOW US ON

Instagram/dgntattoomag
Face/dgn-tattoo-magazine

WWW.DGNTATTOOMAG.COM

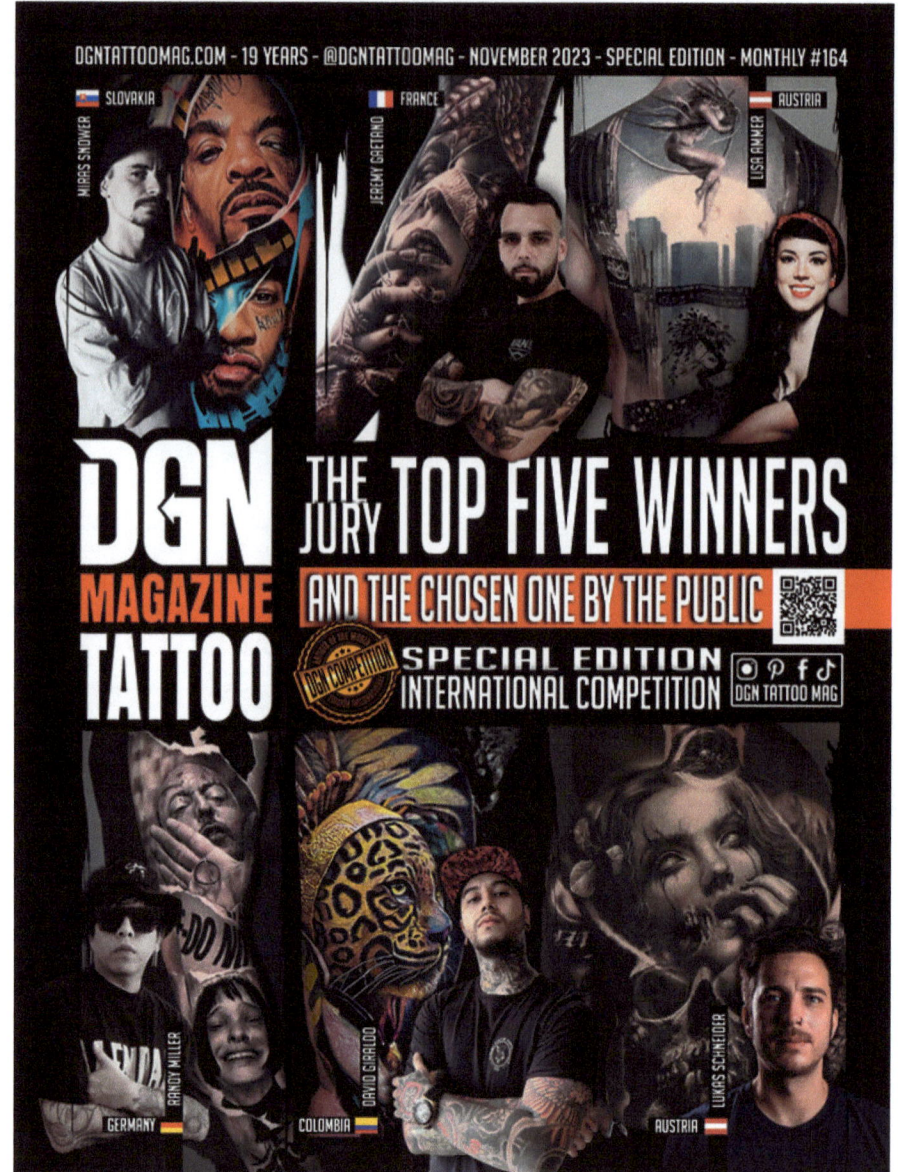

Editor:
Sebastian Harbaruk
dgntattoomag@gmail.com

Editorial Creative Laboratory:
DGN TATTOO
Laprida 151, B1832HOC
Green Corridor Canning / San Vicente
Country Club S/N

International Distribution:

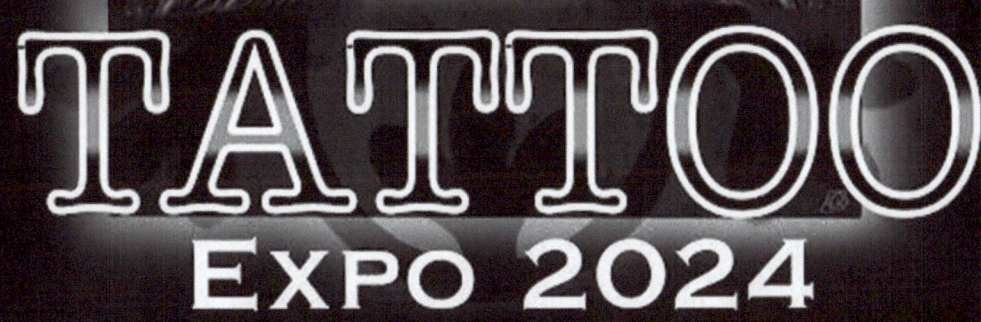

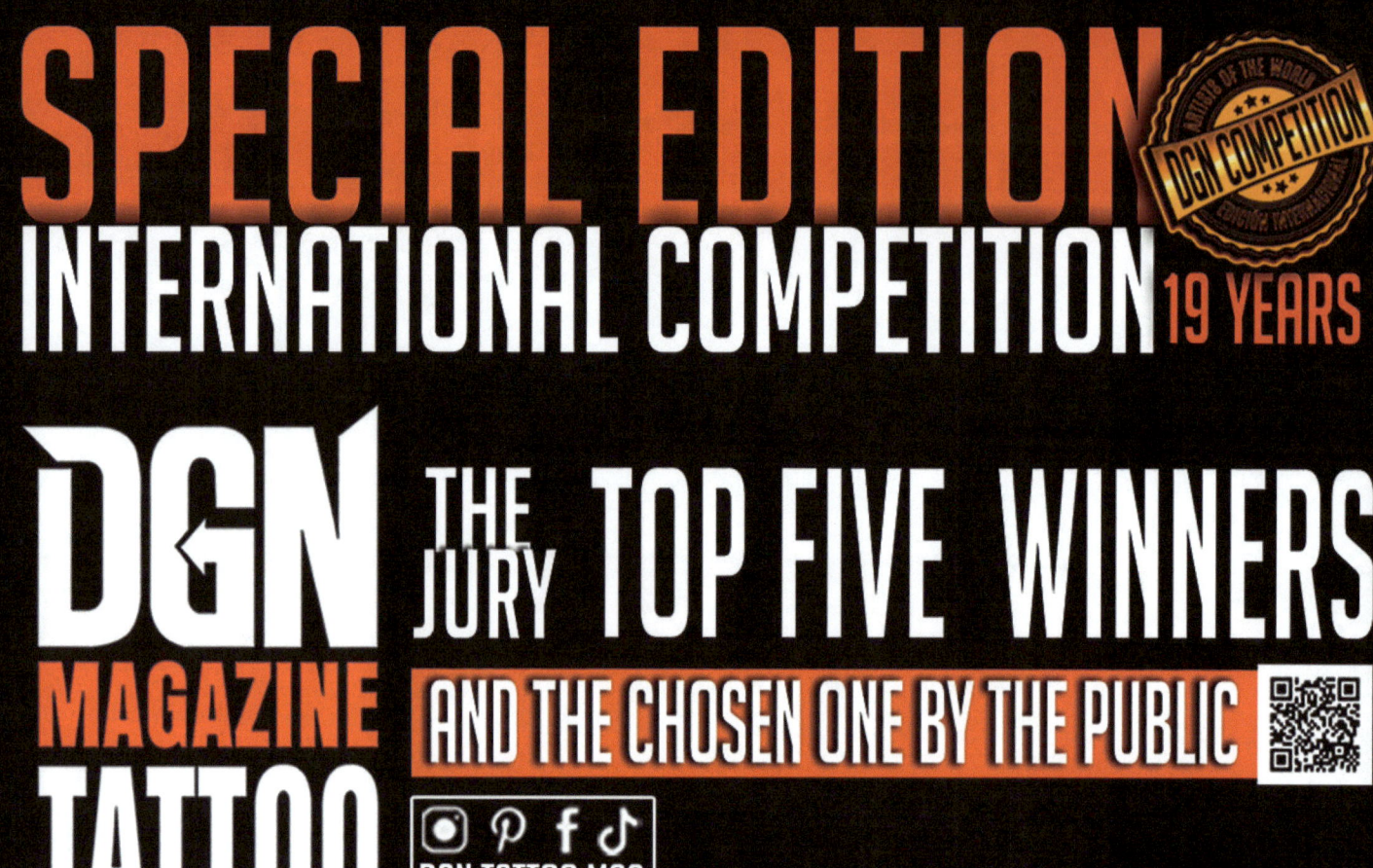

SPECIAL EDITION

INTERNATIONAL COMPETITION · 19 YEARS

ARTISTS OF THE WORLD · DGN COMPETITION

DGN
MAGAZINE
TATTOO

THE JURY · **TOP FIVE WINNERS**

AND THE CHOSEN ONE BY THE PUBLIC

DGN TATTOO MAG

Welcome to a special edition of DGN TATTOO MAGAZINE! On this occasion, we celebrate the winners of the international competition that has captivated tattoo enthusiasts worldwide. Lisa Ammer , Lukas Schneider , Jeremy Gaetano , Randy Miller , and Snower stand out as the TOP FIVE, chosen by our distinguished panel of judges, composed of prominent figures in the world of tattooing, such as Valentina Riabova, Myke Chambers, Victor Portugal, Dave Paulo, Andrei Stepanov, and Haewall. Furthermore, we cannot overlook David Giraldo , the winner selected by the audience as their favorite artist among 130 contestants, who also deserves a prominent place in this special edition. Not only did he captivate the audience, but the panel of judges recognized him as the first-place winner in the versatile category, an impressive achievement that highlights his skill in tattooing. In this special edition, these talented artists will share their beginnings, their experiences in the competition, and their exciting plans for the future. Get ready to immerse yourself in the thrilling world of tattoo art with the best of the competition!

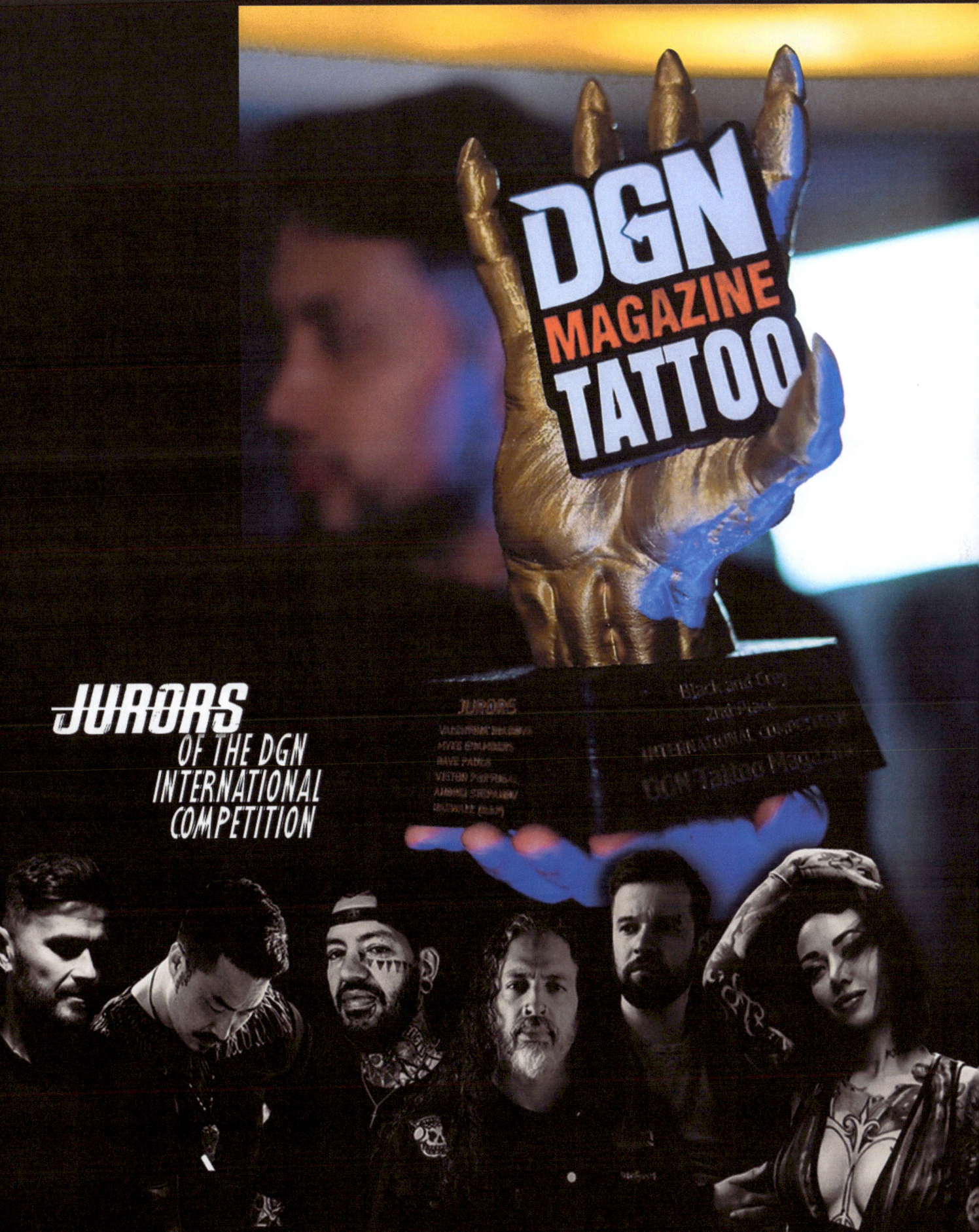

DGN
MAGAZINE
TATTOO

JURORS
OF THE DGN
INTERNATIONAL
COMPETITION

DAVE PAULO - HAEWALL - MYKE CHAMBERS - VICTOR PORTUGAL - ANDREI STEPANOV - VAL RIABOVA

KLAGENFURT / AUSTRIA - @lukas.schneider.tattoo

LUKAS SCHNEIDER

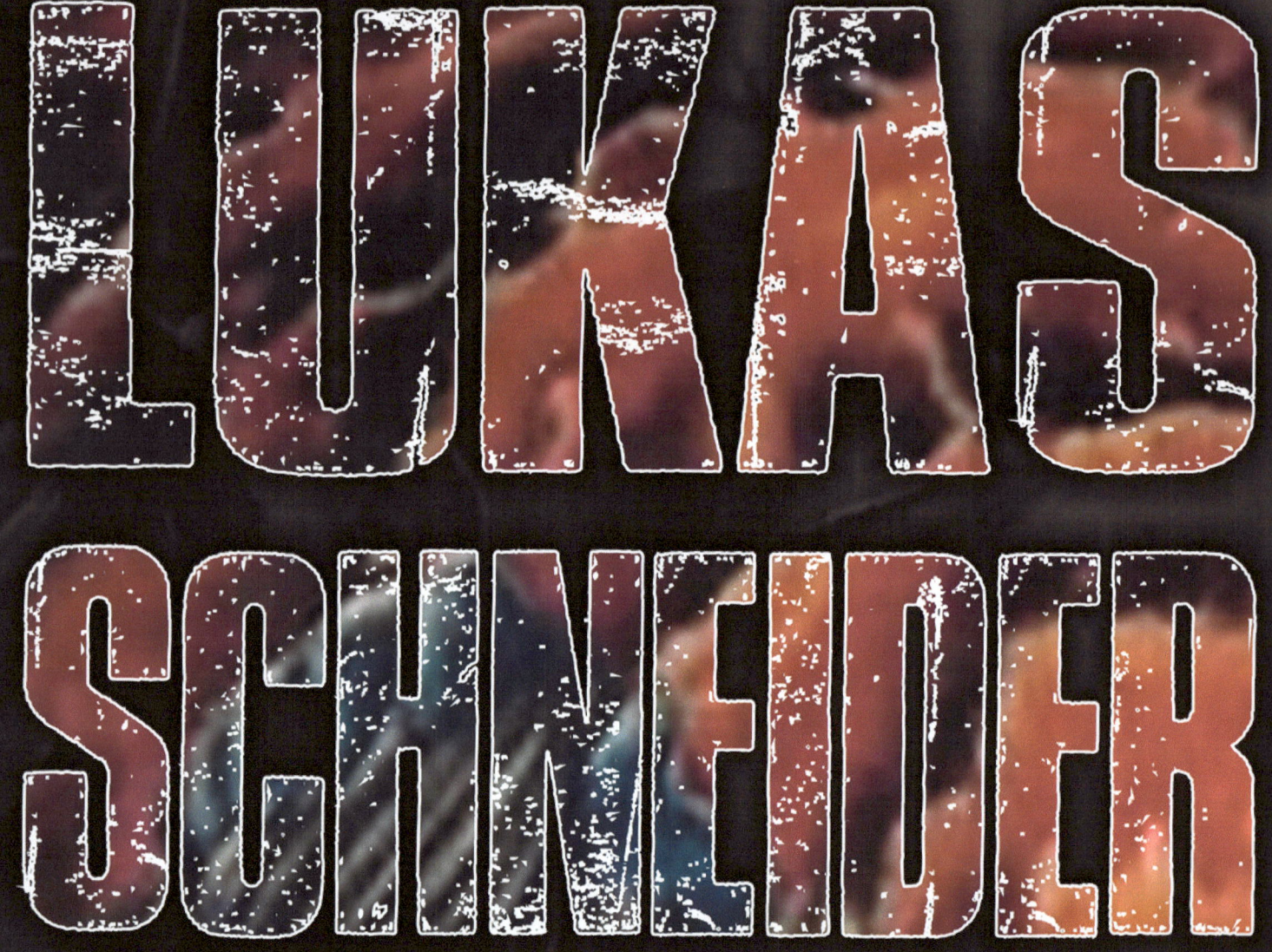

"Acclaimed Austrian tattoo artist specializing in black and grey and color realism, awarded as one of the top 5 tattoo artists in the international competition DGN TATTOO MAGAZINE and consecrated as one of the top 10 artists voted by the public among 130 participants from around the world."

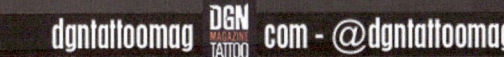

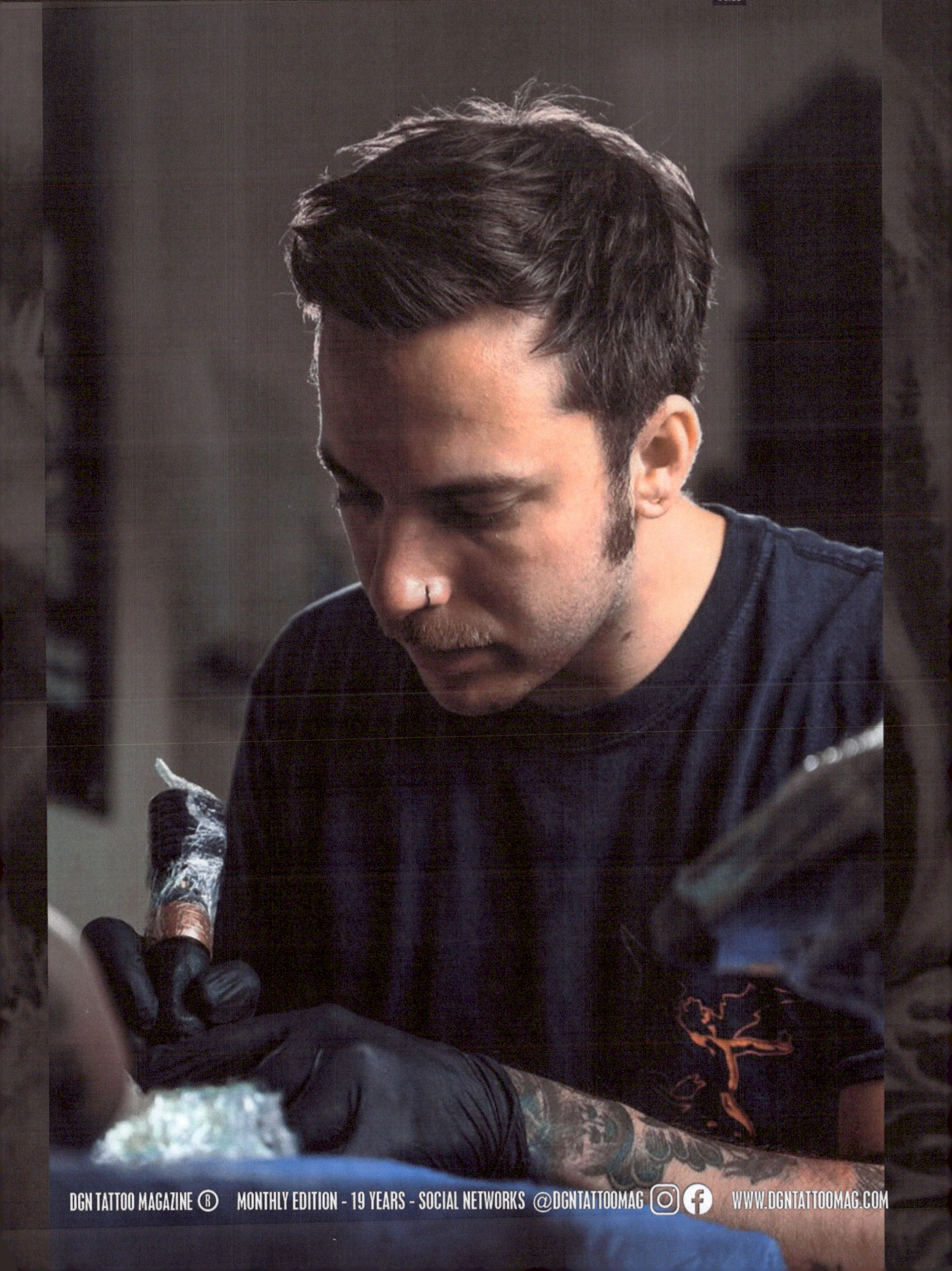

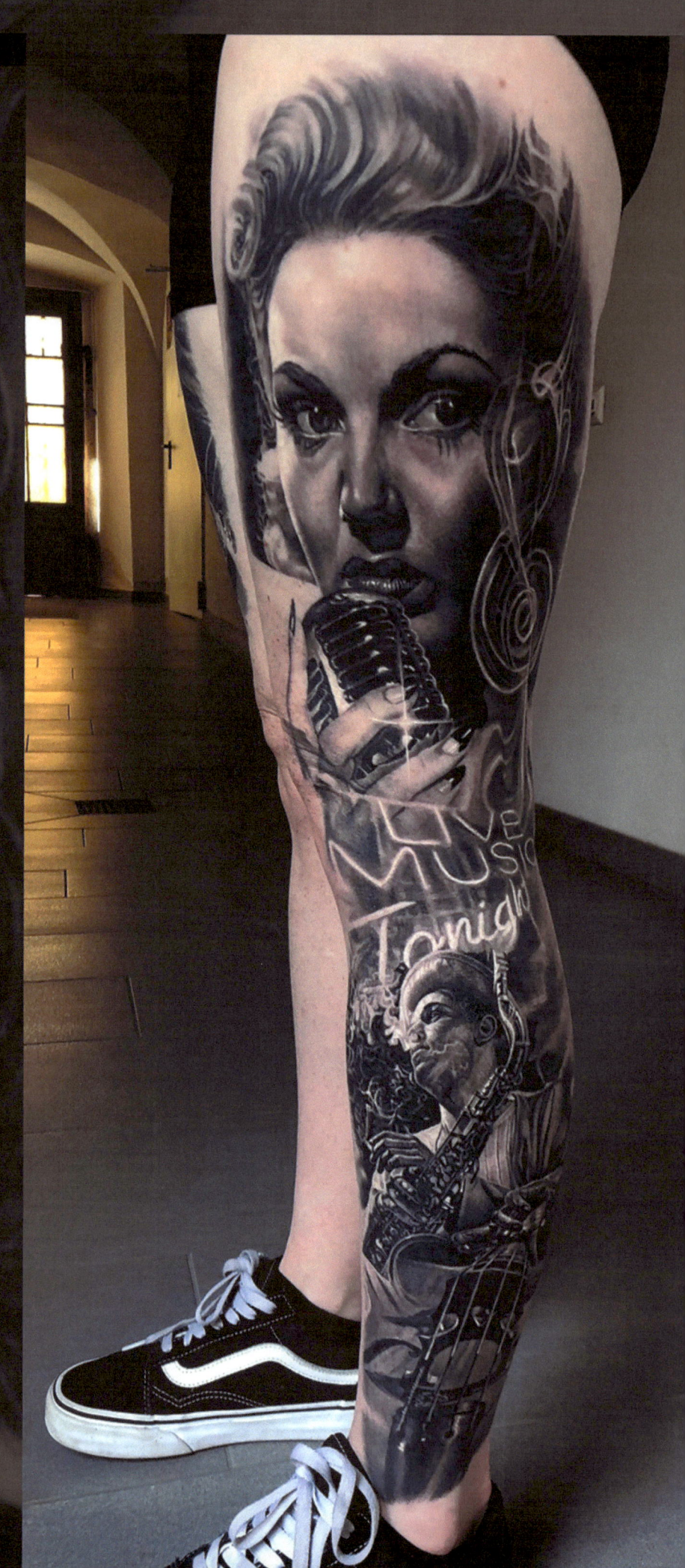

Lukas Schneider is not only an exceptional tattoo artist; he is a master of both black and grey and color realism. This Austrian tattooist has taken the world of tattoo art to new heights with his extraordinary talent and unparalleled skills. Recently, he was recognized as one of the top 5 tattoo artists in the prestigious international competition DGN TATTOO MAGAZINE. The jury, composed of renowned personalities with worldwide recognition, such as Valentina Riabova, Myke Chambers, Dave Paulo, Victor Portugal, Andrei Stepanov, and Haewall, acknowledged Lukas Schneider's exceptional talent.

Born in 1987 in southern Austria, Lukas began his journey into the world of tattooing in 2005. His humble beginnings involved tasks such as soldering needles and cleaning tubes, but his passion and determination led him to become a true master of his craft.

During his early days in the industry, Lukas honed his skills by creating a wide variety of tattoos, from stars to arschgeweih. In a short time, he developed his skills in the new school style, but his true passion lay in realism, where he ultimately made his mark.

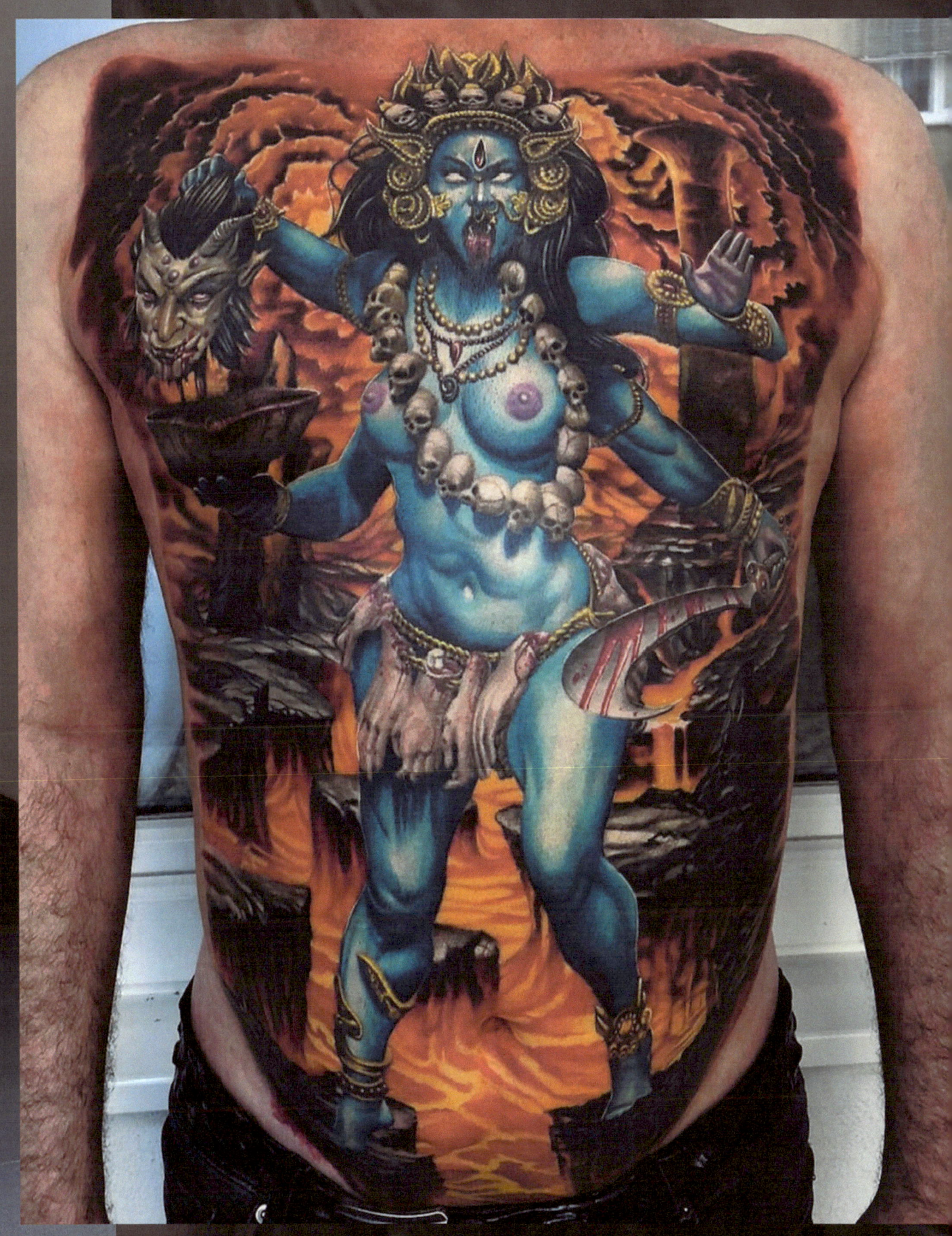

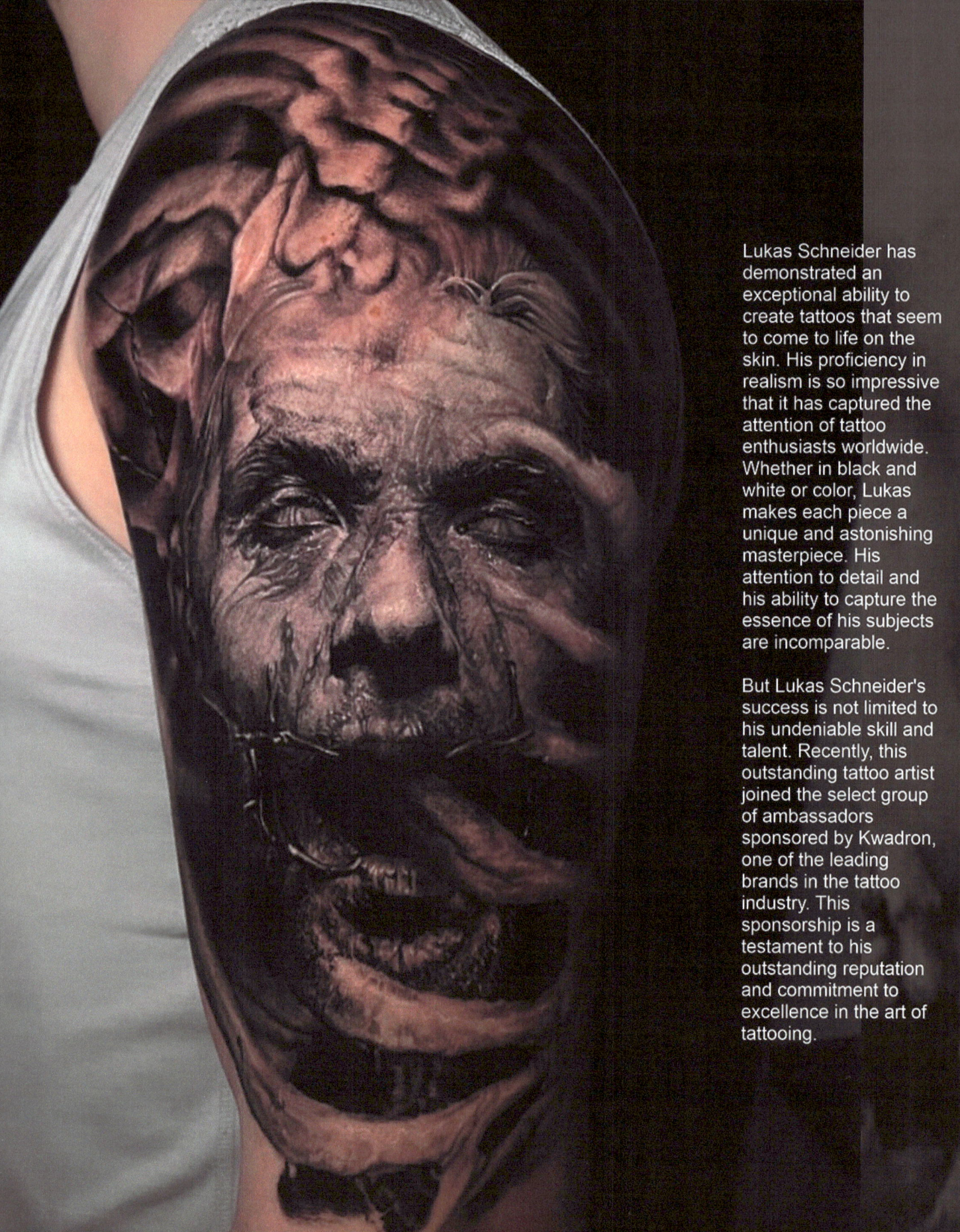

Lukas Schneider has demonstrated an exceptional ability to create tattoos that seem to come to life on the skin. His proficiency in realism is so impressive that it has captured the attention of tattoo enthusiasts worldwide. Whether in black and white or color, Lukas makes each piece a unique and astonishing masterpiece. His attention to detail and his ability to capture the essence of his subjects are incomparable.

But Lukas Schneider's success is not limited to his undeniable skill and talent. Recently, this outstanding tattoo artist joined the select group of ambassadors sponsored by Kwadron, one of the leading brands in the tattoo industry. This sponsorship is a testament to his outstanding reputation and commitment to excellence in the art of tattooing.

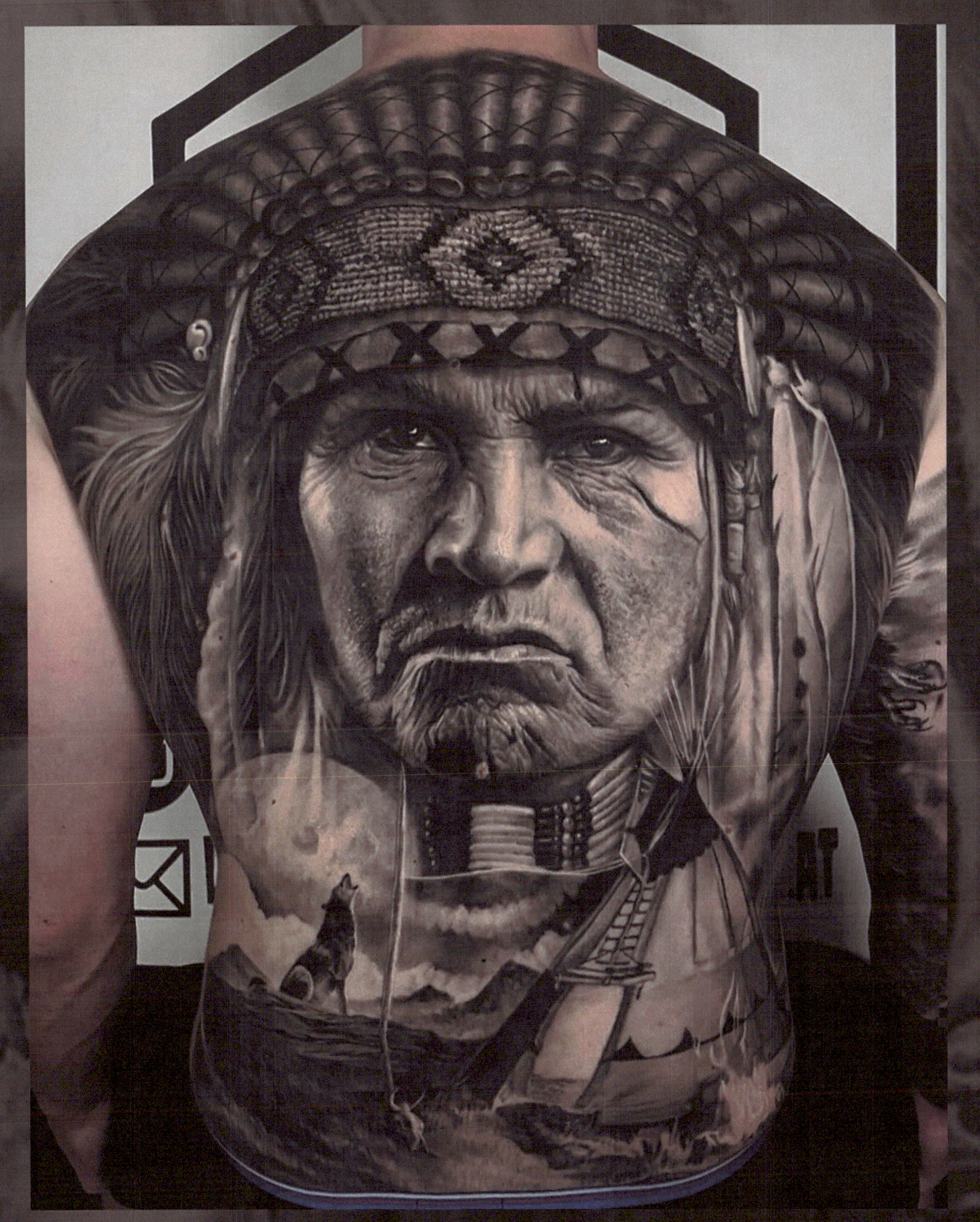

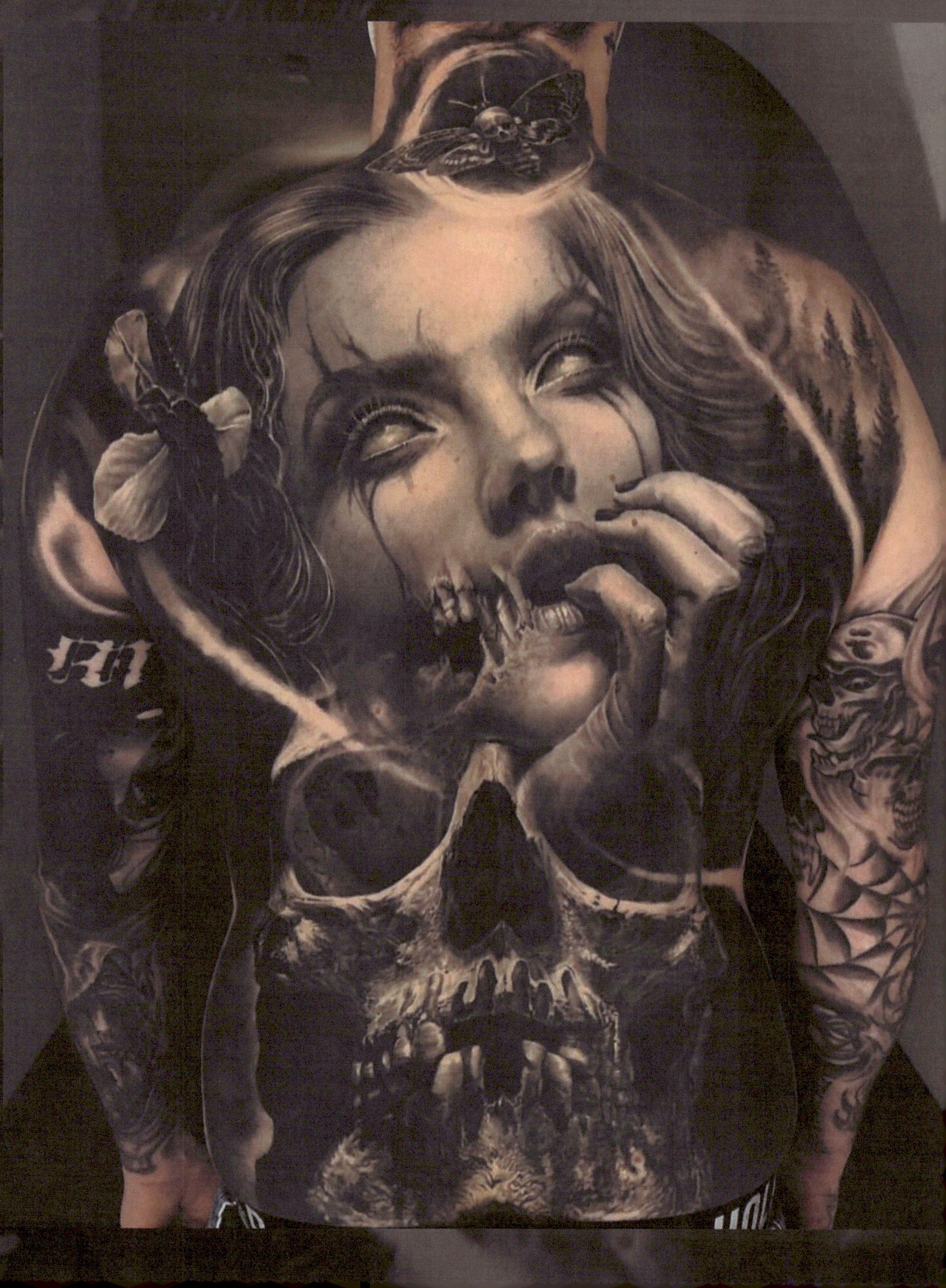

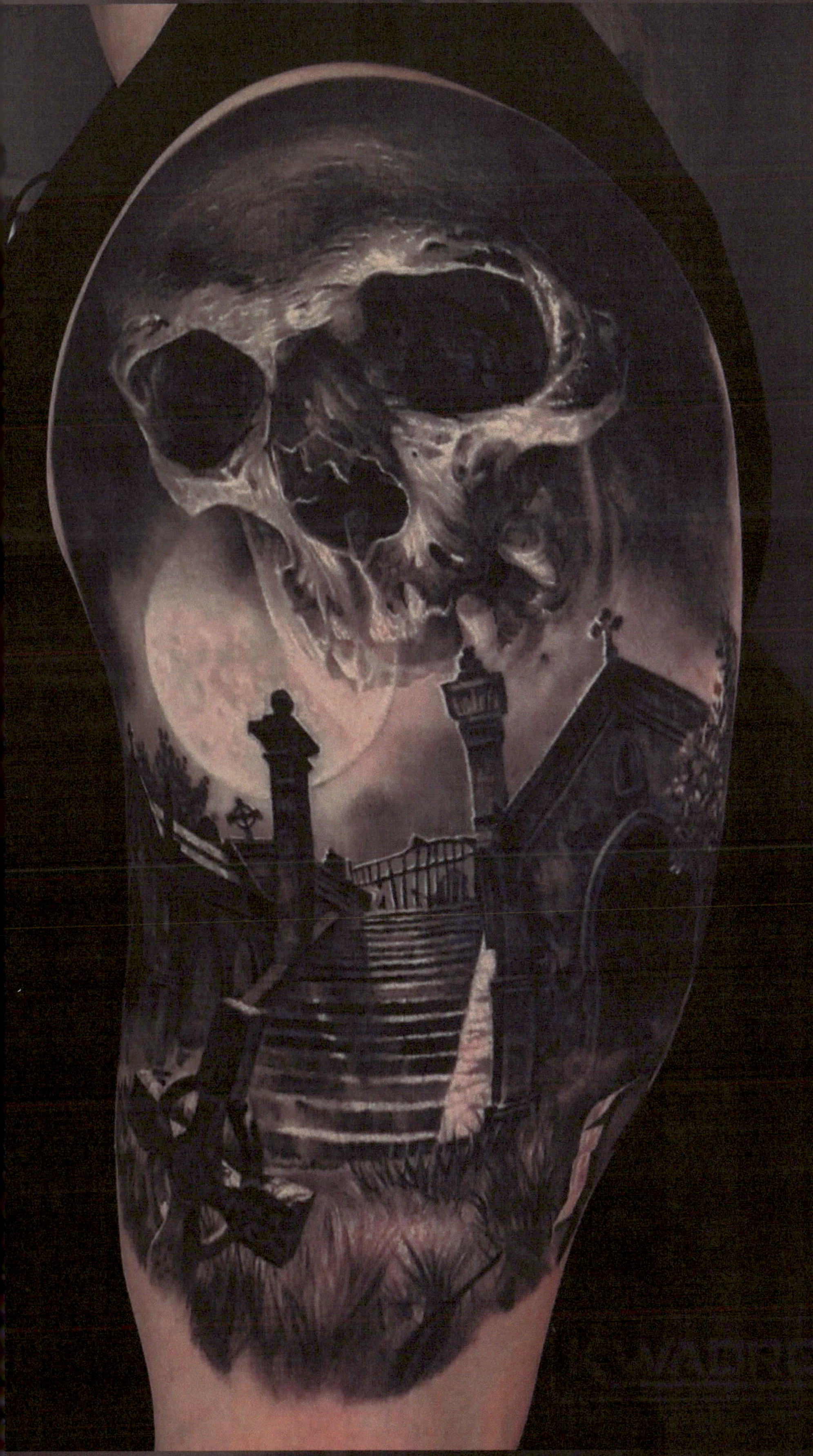

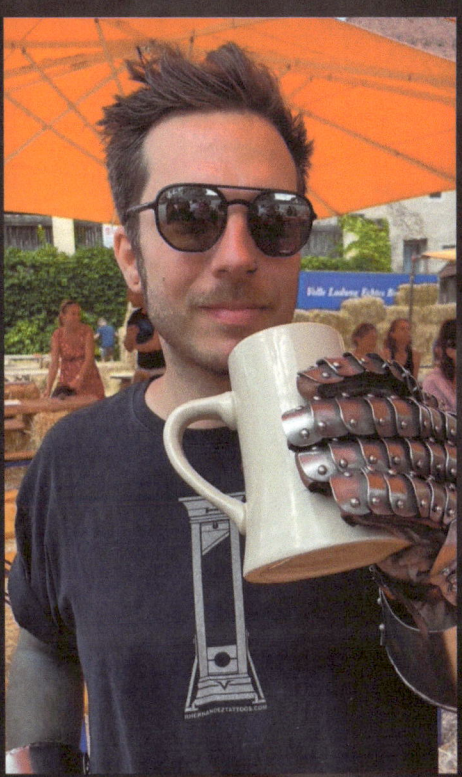

In addition to his success in competitions and the endorsement of significant brands, Lukas Schneider also won the Top Ten award from the public in the same international competition. This distinction set him apart from 130 artists worldwide, establishing him as one of the 10 most voted artists by the public.

Lukas Schneider's legacy continues to grow and evolve as he leaves his mark on the world of tattoo art. As a master of both black and grey and color realism, his work is a constant source of inspiration for colleagues and admirers alike. Keep an eye on this artist, as his journey is far from over, and his art will continue to amaze all those fortunate enough to cross his path.

To stay updated on Lukas Schneider's latest creations and projects, be sure to follow him on his social media channels, @lukas.schneider.tattoo.

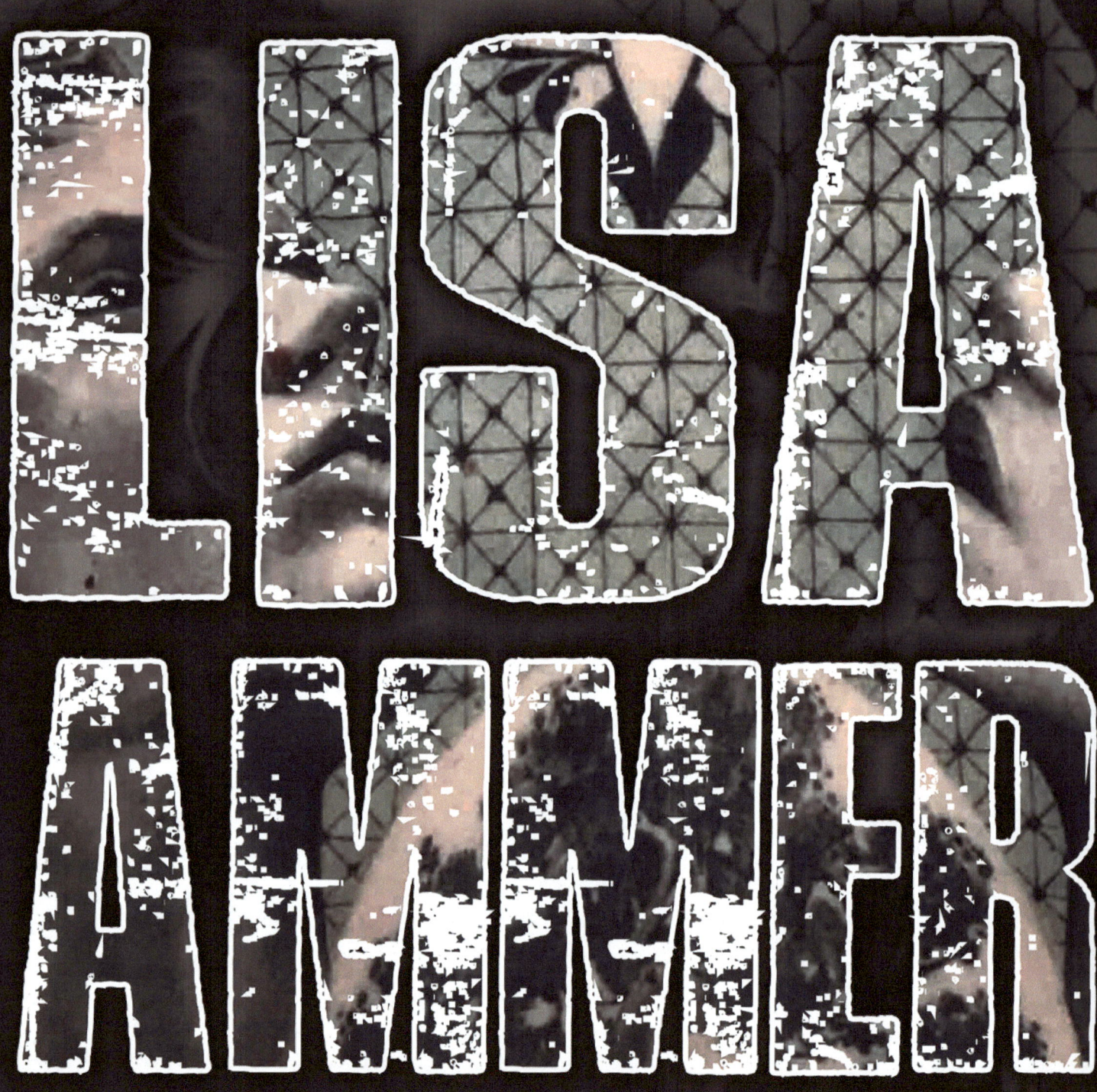

Vienna /Austria - Facebook: lisaammertattoo - Insta: @lisaammertattoo
TikTok: @lisaammertattoo - Website: www.lisaammertattoo.at

LISA
AMMER

Lisa Ammer: A Vanguard Tattoo Artist on the International Body Art Stage

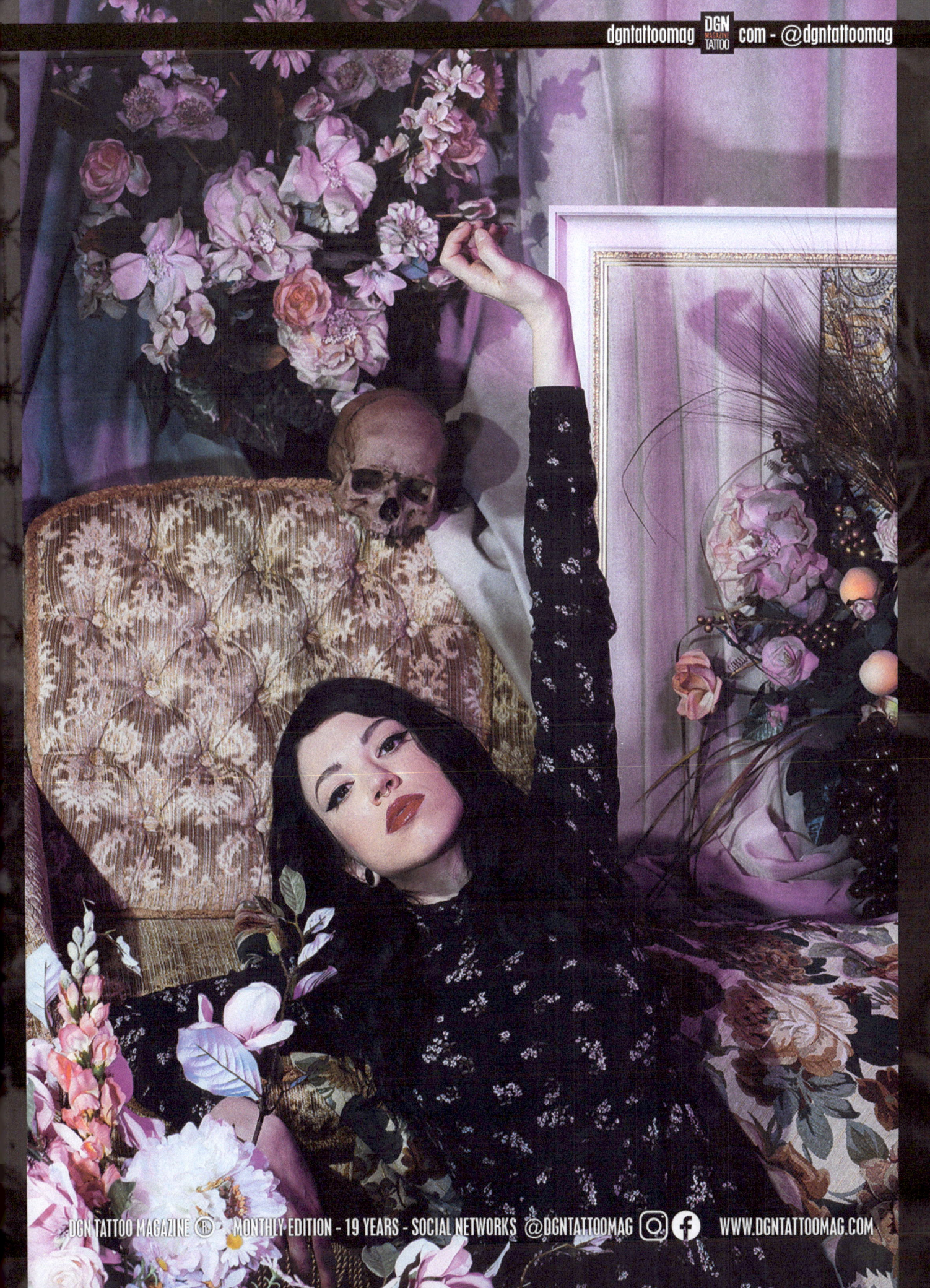

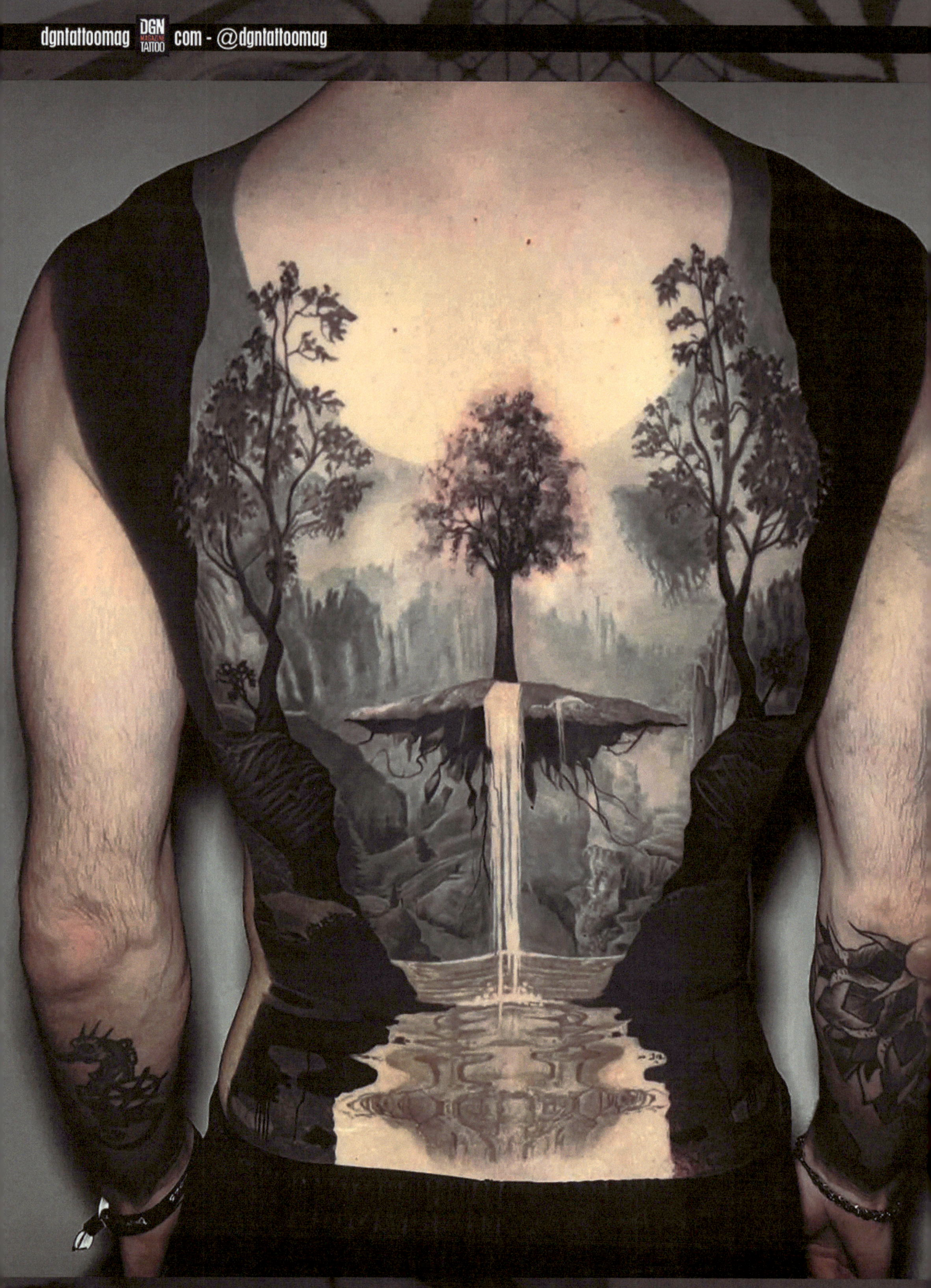

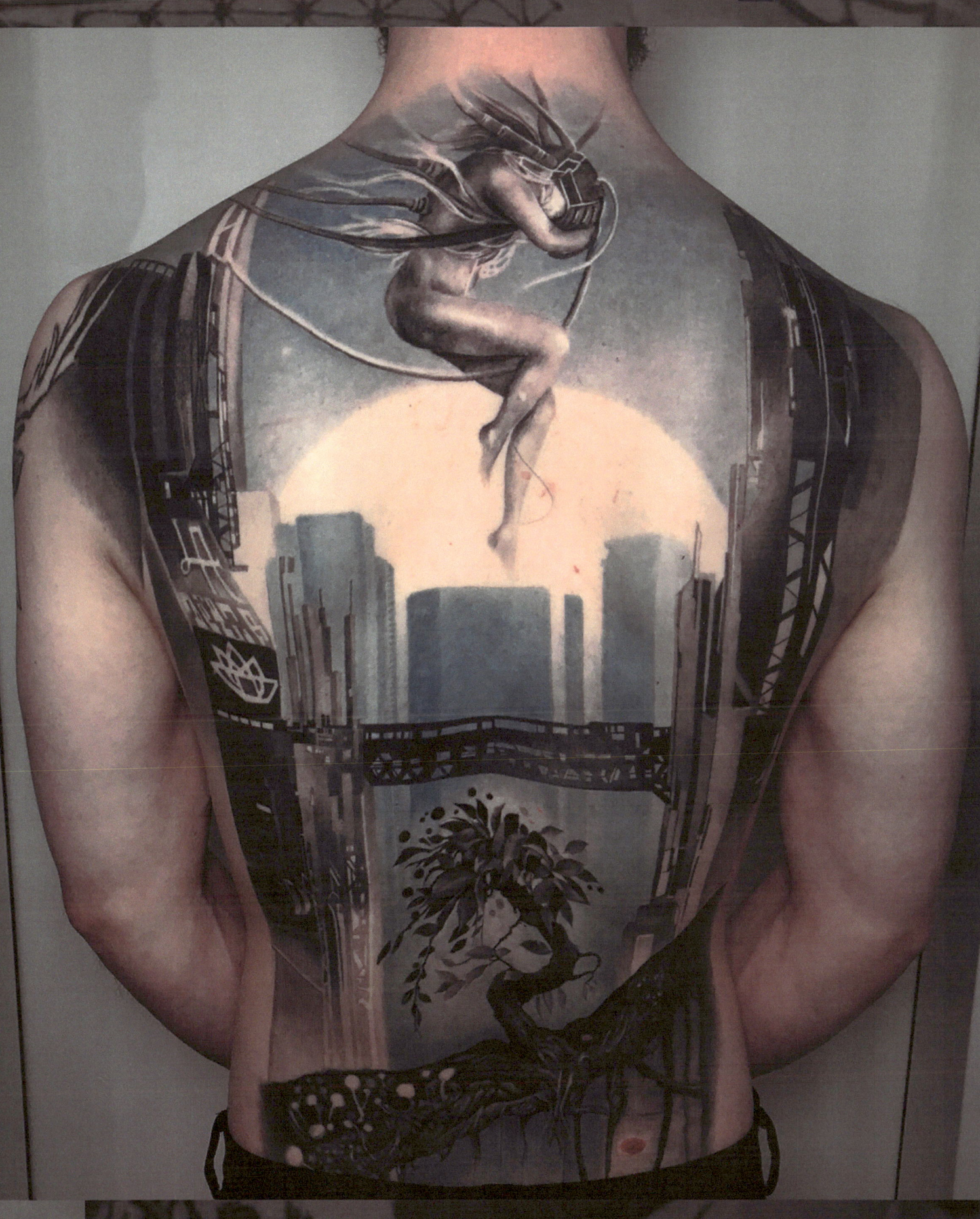

Lisa Ammer, a prominent tattoo artist from Vienna, Austria, has left an indelible mark on the tattoo industry since she began her career in 2011. Currently, she plies her trade as an artist in two renowned studios, "R./ Tattoo X Barber" in Vienna and "Neonjudas" in Berlin, Germany. However, what truly sets Lisa apart is her unique and ever-evolving style that transcends the "Black and Gray" label by incorporating subtle color tones in the background.

Lisa is drawn to the concepts of light and shadow and consistently strives to infuse her work with maximum depth and level grading.

This constant pursuit of artistic perfection led her to participate in the international competition DGN Tattoo Magazine, where she not only joined the top five but was also awarded first place in the prestigious Emerging Art category, as judged by the panel of excellence composed of Victor Portugal, Myke Chambers, Dave Paulo, Valentina Riabova, Andrei Stepanov, and Haewall.

What further highlights her achievement in DGN is that Lisa was chosen by the public, in an eager audience that followed the voting closely on Instagram.

Her ability to captivate a broad base of followers and be among the top ten most voted artists is a testament to the love and admiration her followers hold for her.

With a style that fuses realistic technique and the play of light and shadow, Lisa creates tattoos that transcend mere representation and delve into the realm of art.

Her focus on creating unique and personal pieces rather than directly copying images is a testament to her passion and commitment to her art. While many of her tattoos are in black and white, Lisa also incorporates color tones in the background, adding an extra dimension to her work.

This interplay between lights and shadows, realism, and elements of color sets her work apart and positions her at the forefront of contemporary body art.

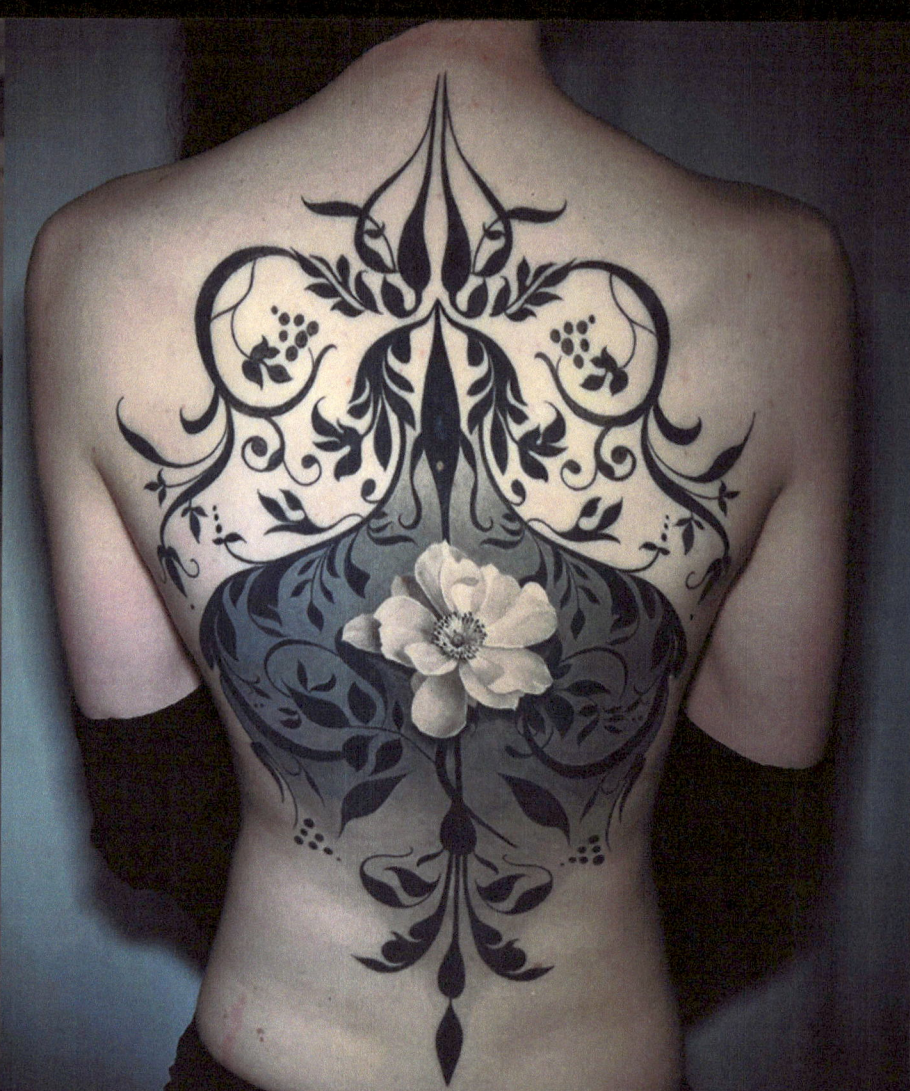

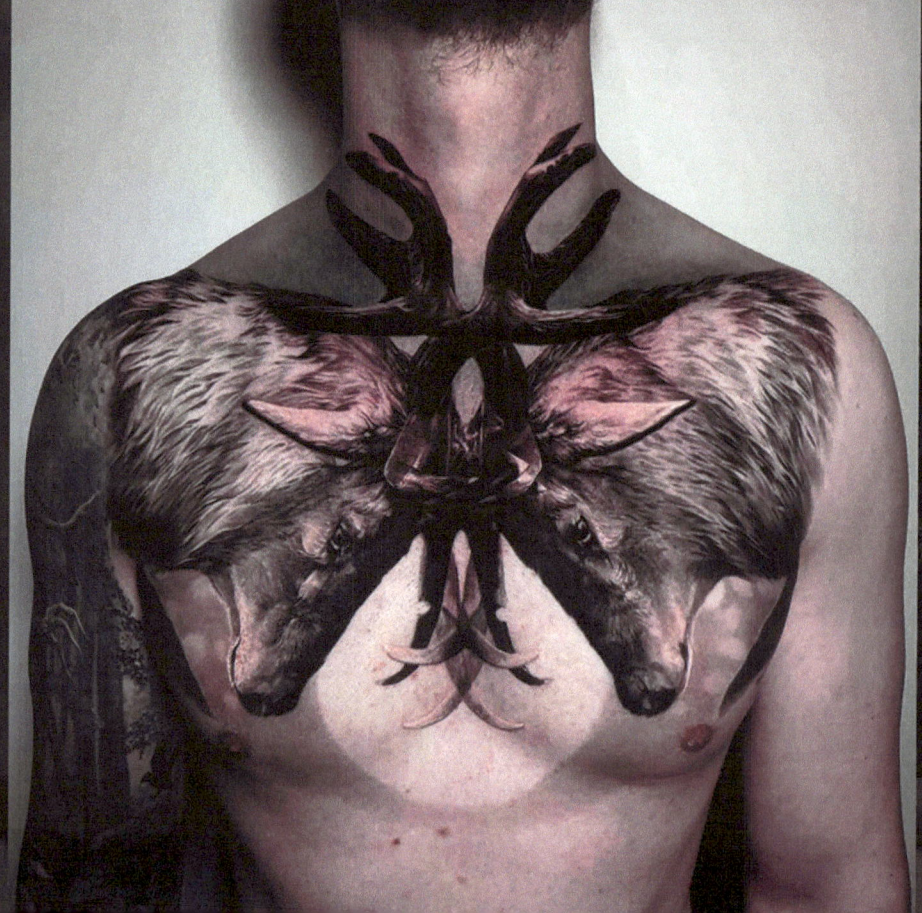

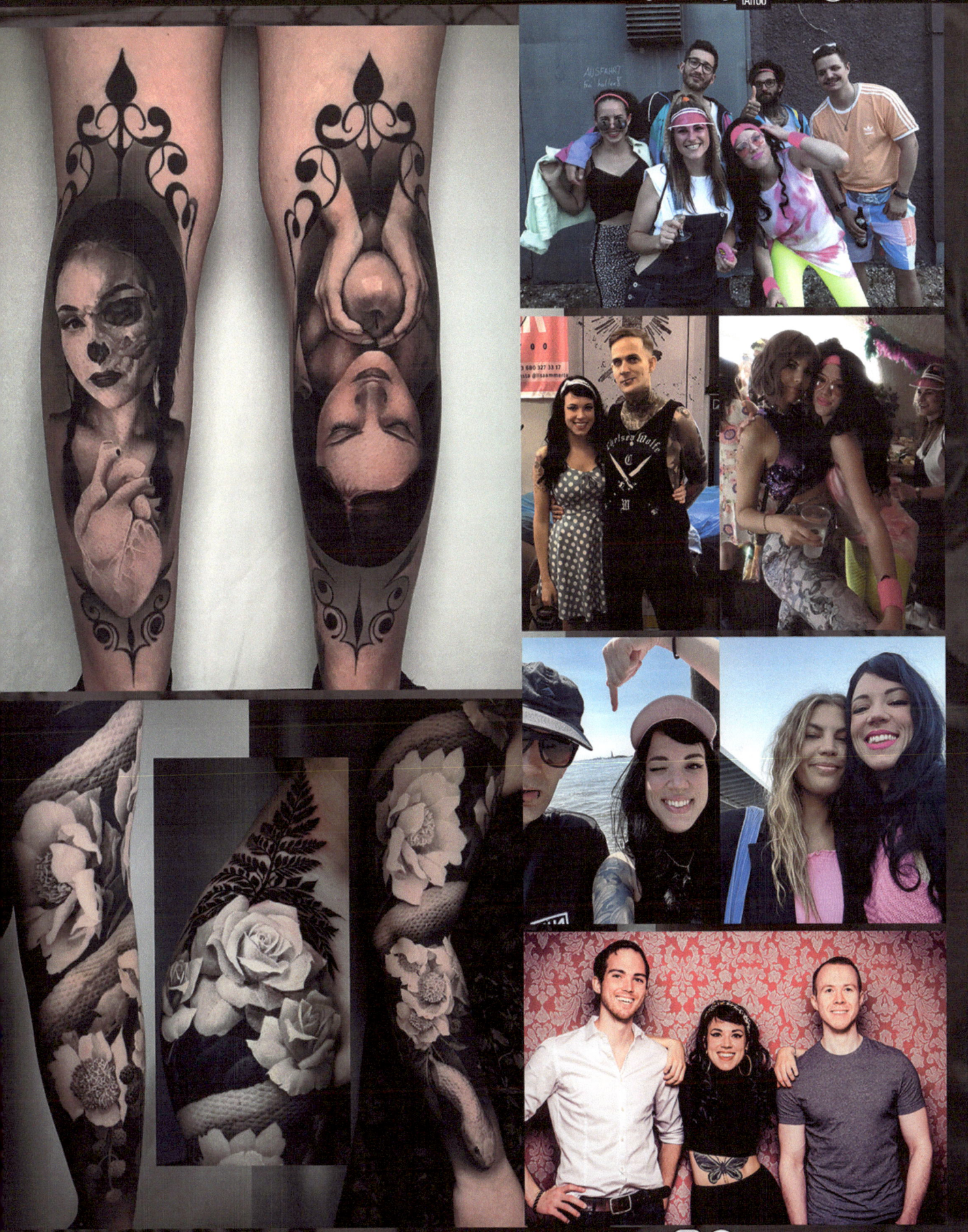

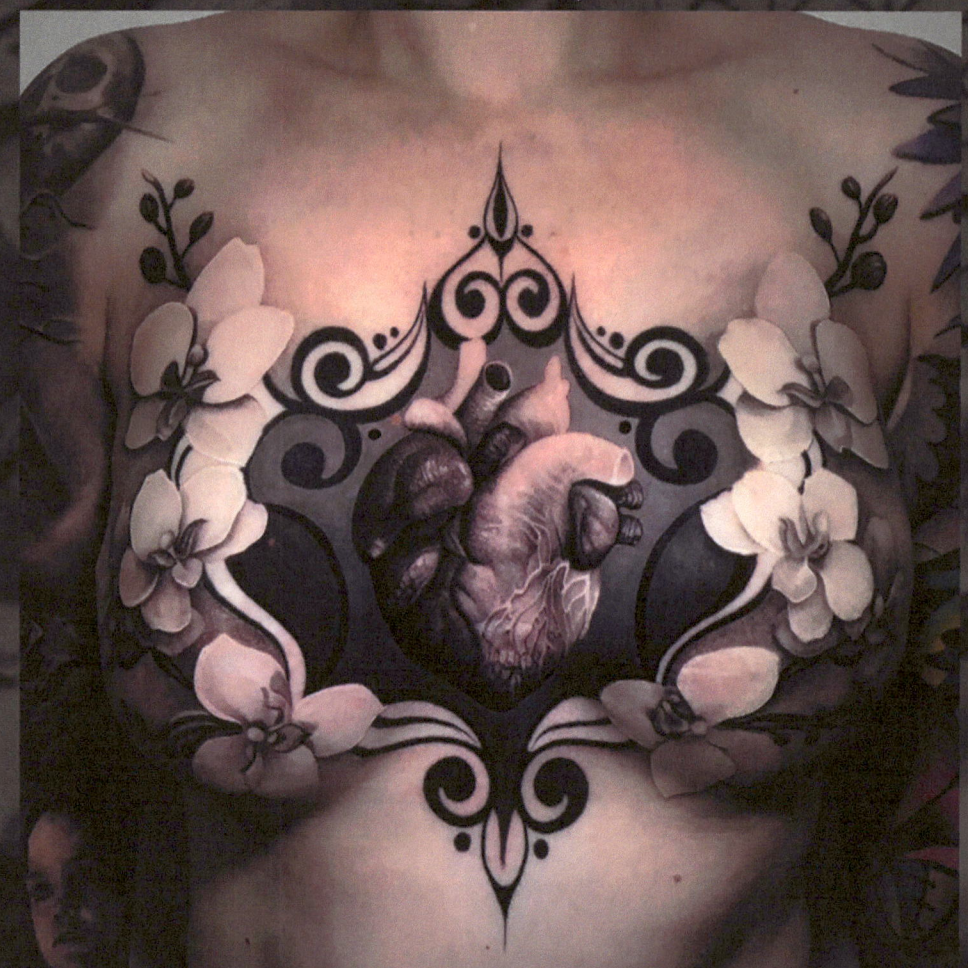

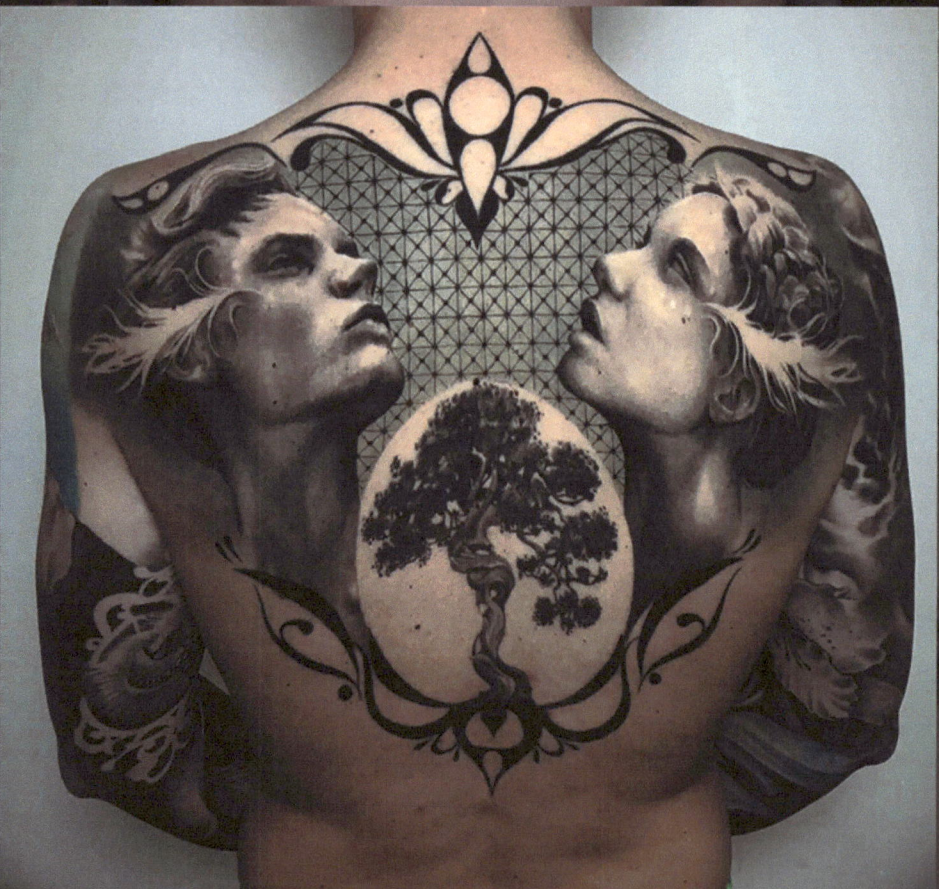

Lisa's studio in Vienna, "R./ Tattoo X Barber," is a hub of creativity and artistic expression.

Here, she collaborates with other tattoo artists and creates an environment conducive to innovation and experimentation.

Her passion for tattooing and her desire to take her art to the next level are reflected in every tattoo she creates.

Lisa also ventures beyond Vienna and has been invited as an artist at the "Neonjudas" tattoo studio in Berlin, Germany.

This allows her to interact with an international audience and share her art with a wide range of tattoo enthusiasts.

Despite her growing success and recognition, Lisa Ammer remains humble and grateful.

Her participation in the international DGN Tattoo Magazine competition and her achievements in the contest are a reflection of her passion and commitment to body art.

With every tattoo she creates, she continues to challenge herself and explore new frontiers in the world of tattooing.

Lisa's future as a tattoo artist promises to be bright.

Her distinctive style and focus on creativity and artistic expression make her an influential figure in the tattoo community.

Tattoo enthusiasts, both in Vienna and abroad, can eagerly anticipate her future masterpieces.

Lisa Ammer has become a vanguard artist on the international body art stage, and her impact will endure for generations.

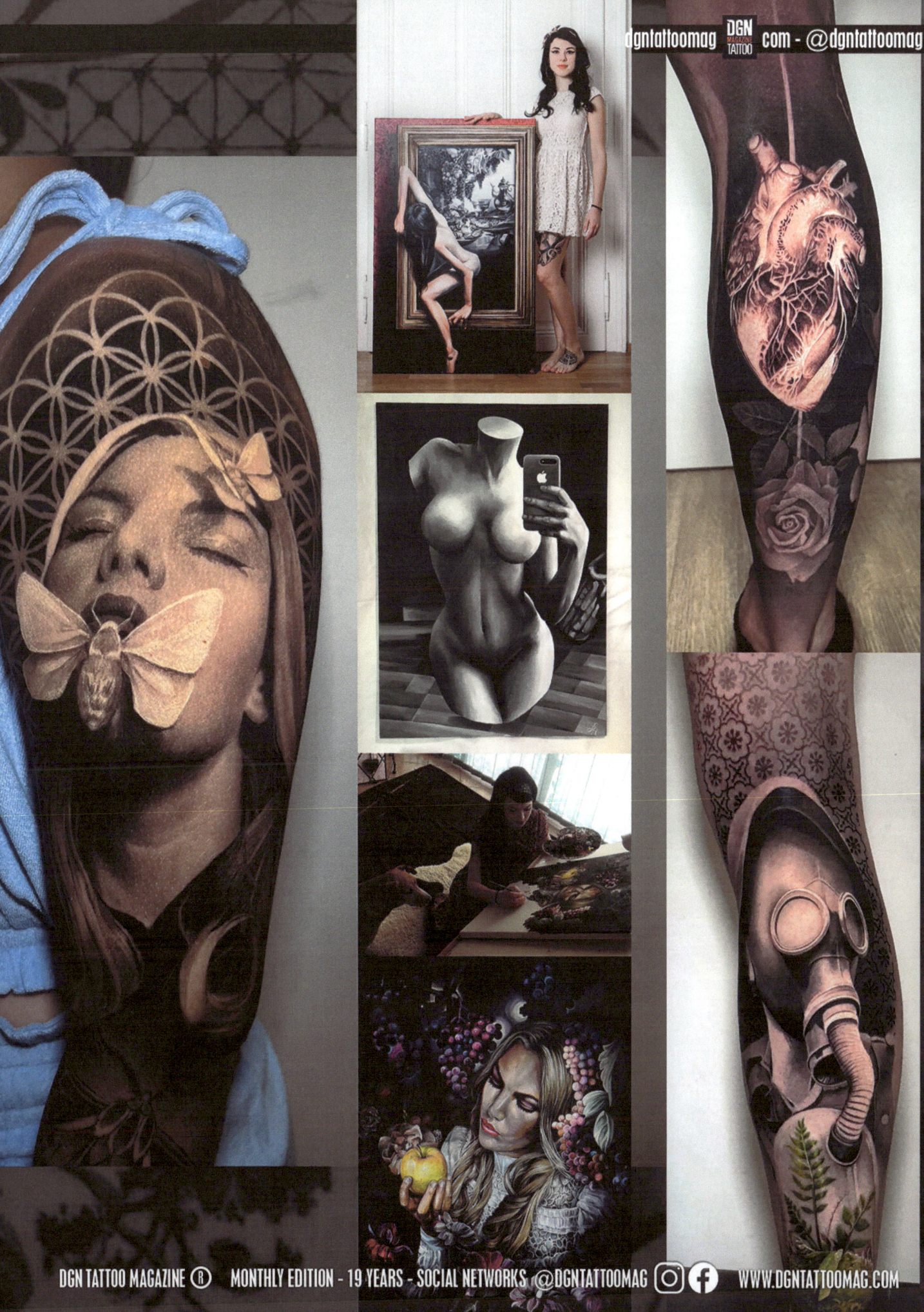

Sanary / France - @Gaetano_tattoo - Tattoo Studio: Nuance Noire

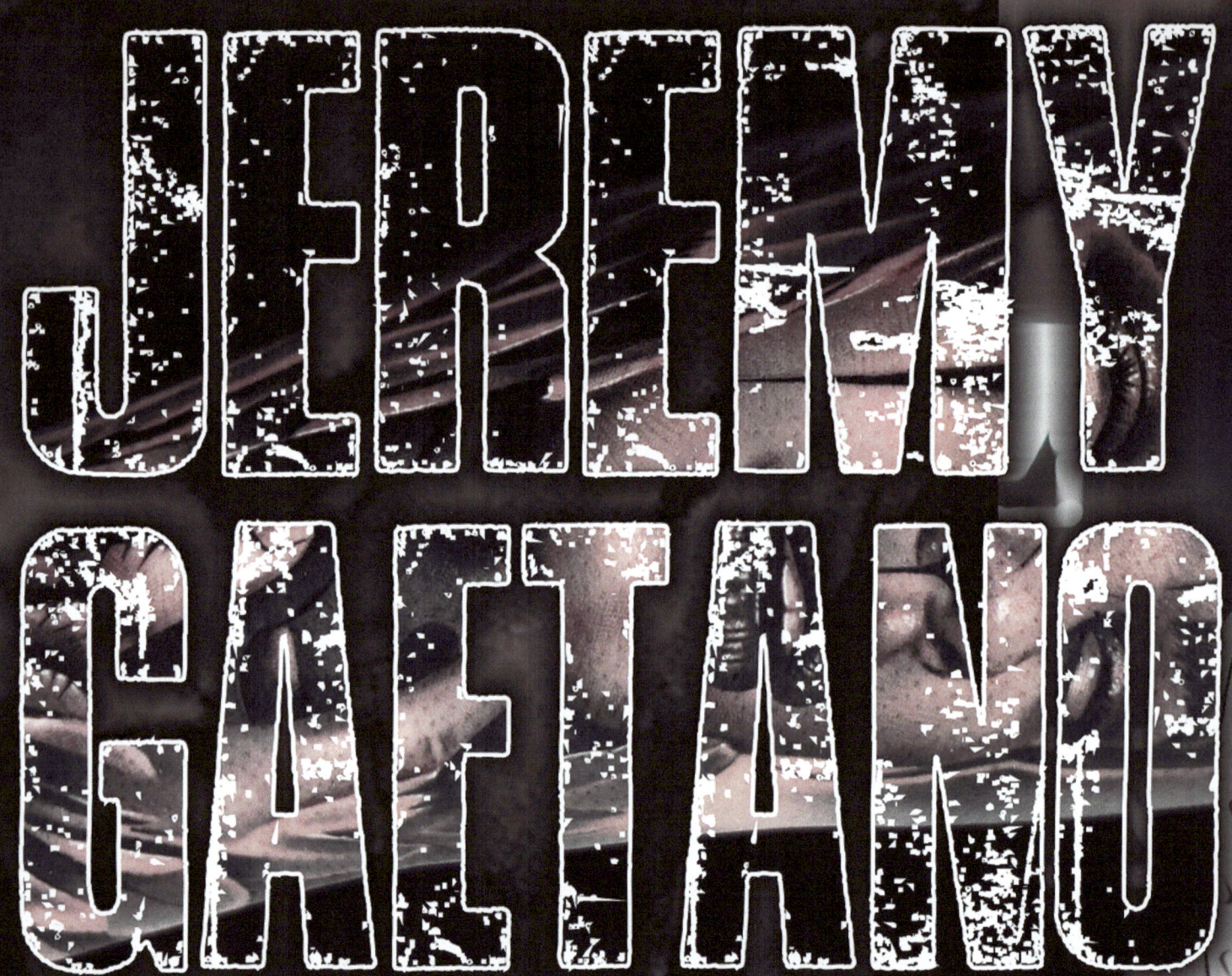

JEREMY GAETANO

"Exploring the World of Realism in Tattoo Art"
In this captivating interview, we delve into the world of tattooing and discover how art intertwines with Gaetano's life, a talented tattoo artist based in Sanary, France. With a focus on realism, Gaetano shares his experiences from his early days of drawing to his success in the international DGN Tattoo Mag competition. What drove him to become a tattoo artist? How did hip-hop culture influence his art? Join us on a journey through his career, his passion, and his vision for the future in the world of tattooing.

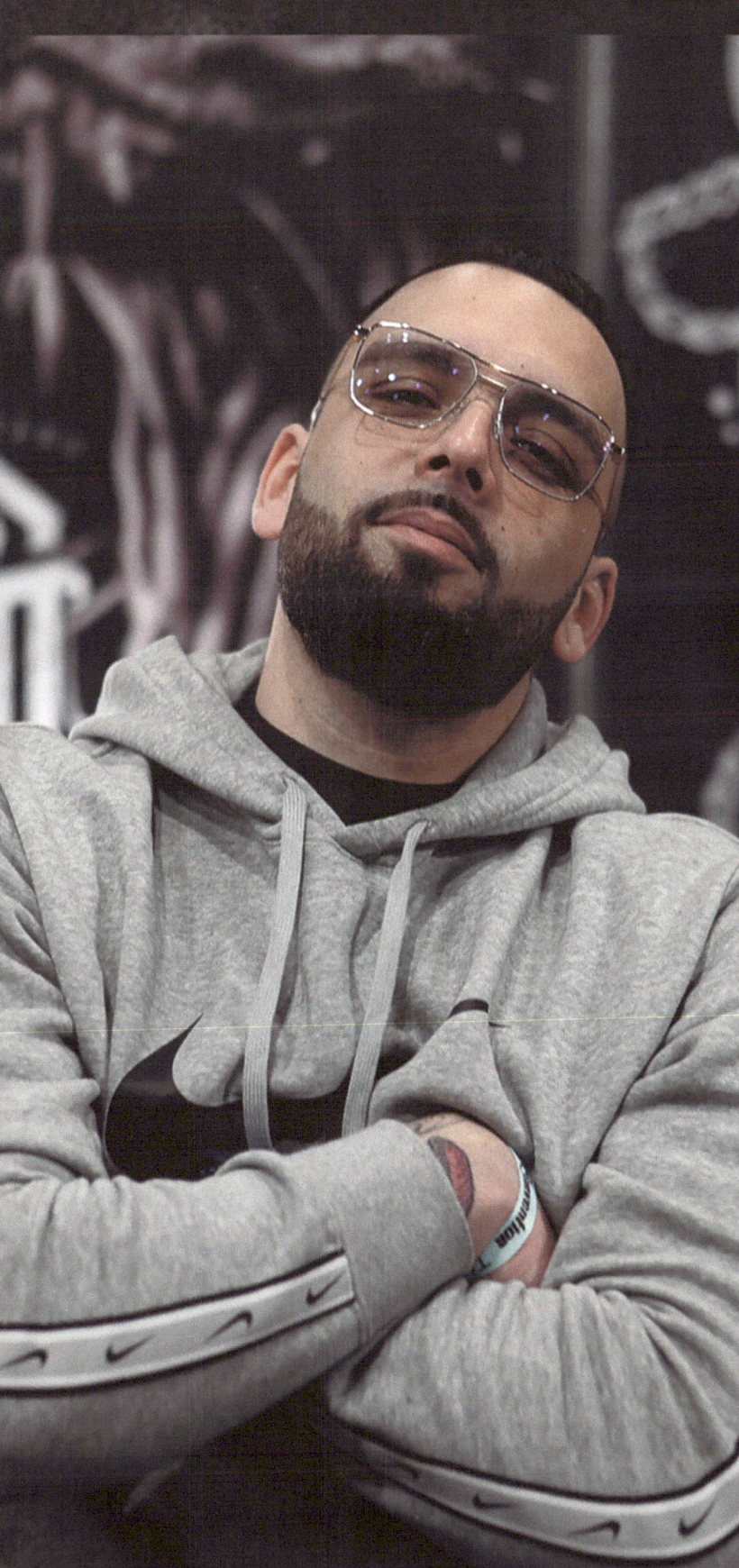

1.How did your interest in art begin?From a young age, you were interested in drawing. How do you think this passion influenced your career as a tattoo artist?

Since I was a kid I was very attracted in drawing, I spent hours in my bedroom doing it. I always had eases.
The fun fact about this is that I was already a fan of realism, textures, animals; 20 years after, I directly turned myself to this when I started tattooing.

2. Let's talk about your transition from graffiti to tattooing.How did hip-hop culture influence your evolution as an artist?

The transition between graffiti and tattoo was not really registered in my artistic approach, I was a very young boy, it was more a claim, a state of mind, a way to deal with all the problems that I had back in the days.
The hip hop culture and the rap music cradled me a lot, I was a 90's kid with all the thing that was contained in it.
When all the kids of my neighborhood were playing soccer, I had crayons in my hand listening to Tupac, Foxy Brown, Notorious BIG and all the biggest rap stars of the moment, I was deeply touched by the different visual aspects contained in the hip hop culture and I think these aspects still influence my choices in tattoo

3. Tell us about your first tattoo.At 18, you got your first tattoo as a client. What motivated you to make the leap and become a tattoo artist?

My first tattoo was a disturbing experience, I had the impression to be another person, I was feeling that I could shape myself in a different way, I was chasing my identity in a very eventful childhood.
At school I've always been misjudged, the teachers always tagged me as a difficult child, that I was, simply because I was misunderstood.
Tattooing became a way to assume my differences.
I became a tattoo artist cause my professional life was sad, I couldn't find my way, I was feeling bad not having a work that captivated me.
Till the day a friend handed me a tattoo machine and since this moment it was an evidence.

4. You made the decision to leave your job and focus on tattooing.What led you to make that decision, and how was the self-taught learning process like?

Yes, I was working on a construction site and I was a security agent too.
When tattoo hit me, I was planning to make a trip to visit my father in Panama, when I landed there I had the

opportunity to work in a tattoo studio with confirmed tattoo artists which allows me to see another tattoo culture, I was feeling really great being a part of the team, I had the impression that I found the perfect work for me. Back in France, I took the decision to stop all the others activities that I had at this moment to focus on tattoo.

I was staying at home from morning to evening, I was drawing everyday and I was tattooing my friends after this.

It began really fast for me, so I professionalized myself, I rented a tiny studio, all I had to do was to prove everybody I was a part of the family

5. You specialize in realism.What attracts you the most to this style, and what challenges have you faced in perfecting it?

I'm attracted by all the emotions that realism can transcribe, from painting to tattoo, realism is a doorway to emotions.

I love to put life in my artworks, a smile, a look, a wince. I surprise myself finding an emotion in a laundry movement or a light passing through some leaves.

The challenge of perfection is still present everyday. I try to question myself everyday on my work, trying to do it the best way that I can.

There is periods that allows it, some doesn't.

Globally I find challenges in every parameters of the art of realistic tattoo.

6. You've participated in several masterclasses to improve your skills.How have these experiences influenced your development as a tattoo artist? Is there a particular lesson you'd like to highlight?

The principal lesson that I take out of it is that you can only count on your own reasoning and your own capacity of evolution.

It's good to get advices from big artists, it can help in the application of new techniques.

You got to keep in mind that nothing is more beneficial that developing your own style with your own codes.

7. You currently work in a private studio in Sanary-sur-Mer, France.What inspires you to keep refining your art, and what is your creative process like?

My inspiration is fed by a lot of things, travels, contest and others, I love to live exciting moments that will stimulate my creativity.

The contests are the best way for me to come back to the studio and try to level up my style.

My creative process is simple, when ideas are coming, I work, I design, I try things that I like but I never forget to

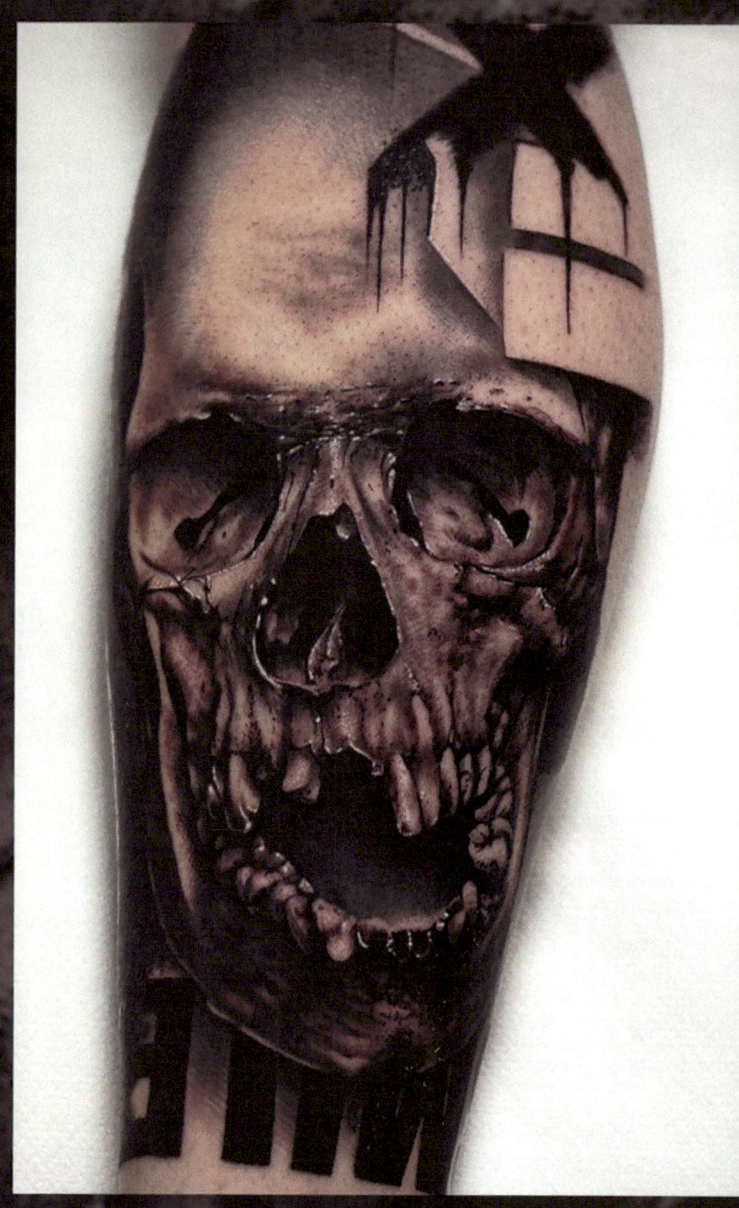

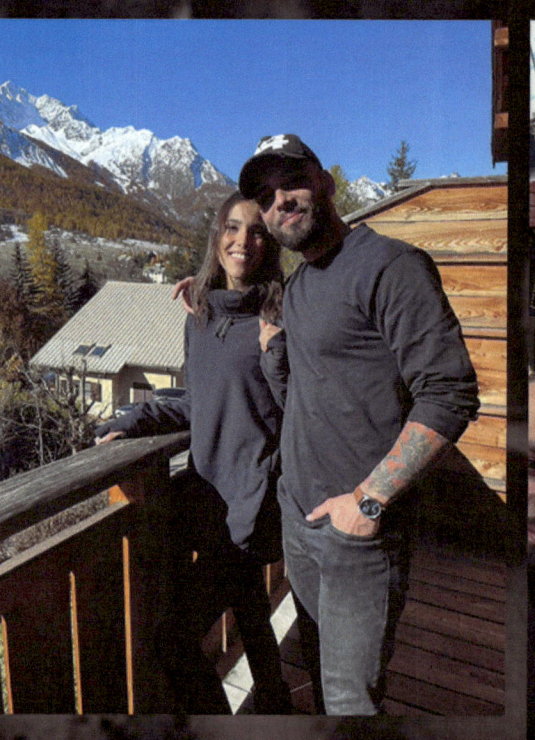

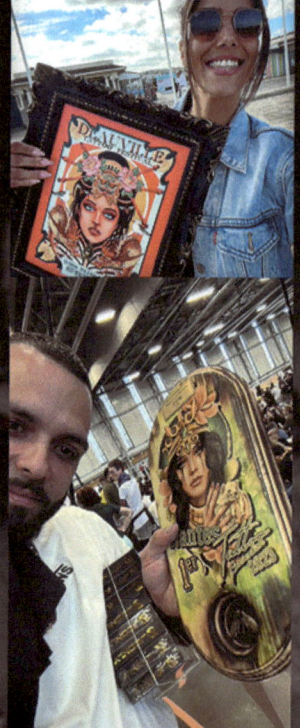

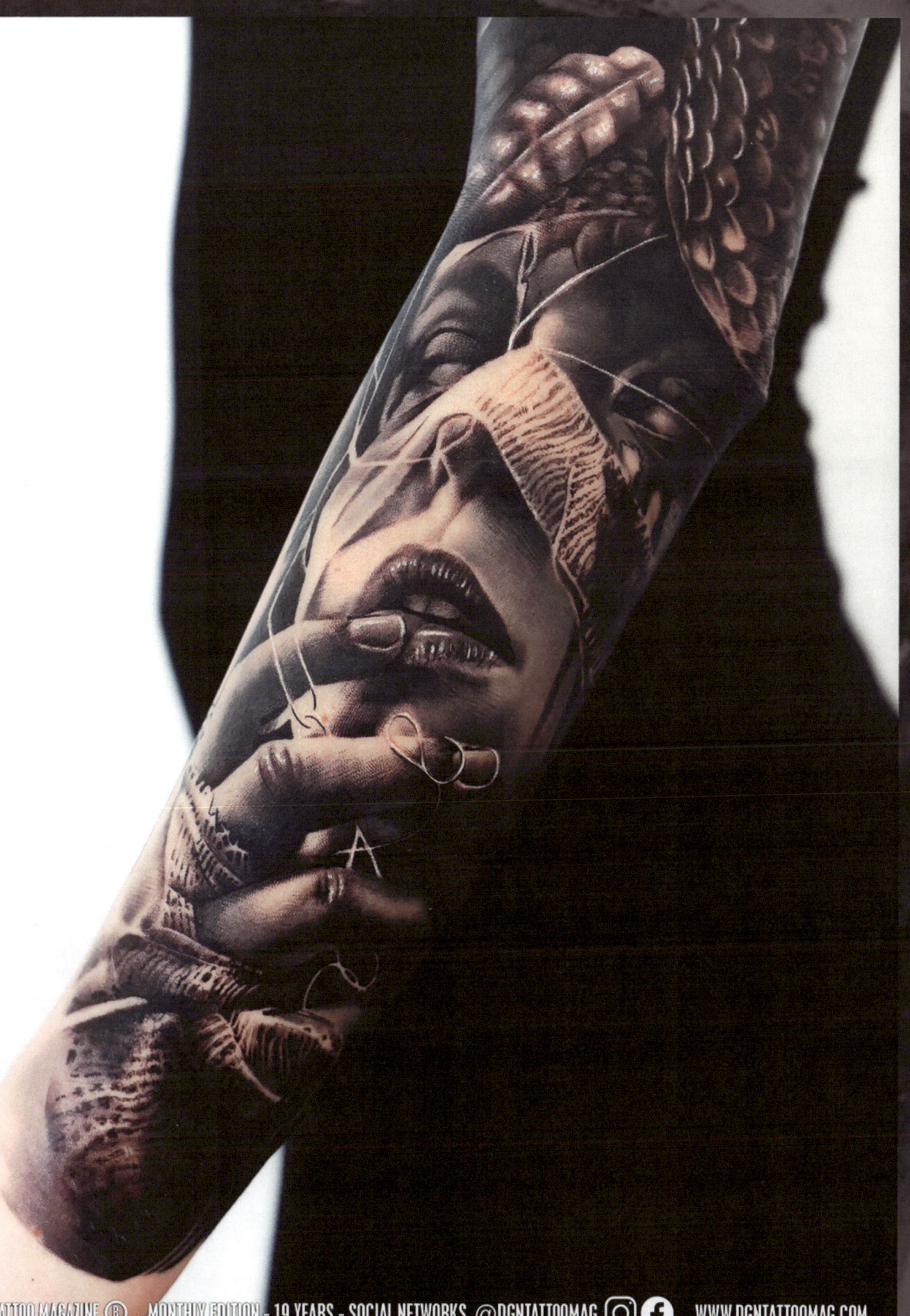

keep my identity first.
I'm tattooing 3 or 4 days a week, trying to save time for the creation and the elaboration of my projects.

8. Let's discuss your participation in the DGN Tattoo Mag international competition. What motivated you to enter?

When DGN sent me a message to participate to the contest I was really flattered, the DGN contest is a serious one, internationally known, the contestants are really good.
I like competition, it allows me to gauge the quality of my work.
It's a beautiful opportunity for me.

9.The jury for this competition consisted of prominent experts.How did you feel knowing that your work would be evaluated by such a high-level jury, including renowned artists?

It's satisfying but frightening at the same time.
When you know that your work will be seen and judged by artists that you love, that you follow, being a top 5 artist is remarkable for me.
The realism category was full of great artists, that's a great honor to be a part of the ranking.
I'm really thankful that the judges liked my work.

10.It was a surprise and an honor to be selected as one of the top 5 artists in the competition.Can you share your emotions and thoughts when you received this news?

I was having dinner with my friends, I took 2 minutes to check my emails, when I saw the first words I've immediately understood that i was selected in the top 5.
I grabbed the magazine to show to my friends all the great artists that was in the competition and told them how happy I was.

11.What do you consider the key to your success in the competition?Was there a specific aspect of your work that you believe impressed the jury?

For me, the key to success, when I'm going to contests, is the Impact.
The first look has to be impactful, big pieces, with hard contrasts.
It's impossible for me to determine which part of my work the judges love the most, maybe just the placement on the body, the proportions.

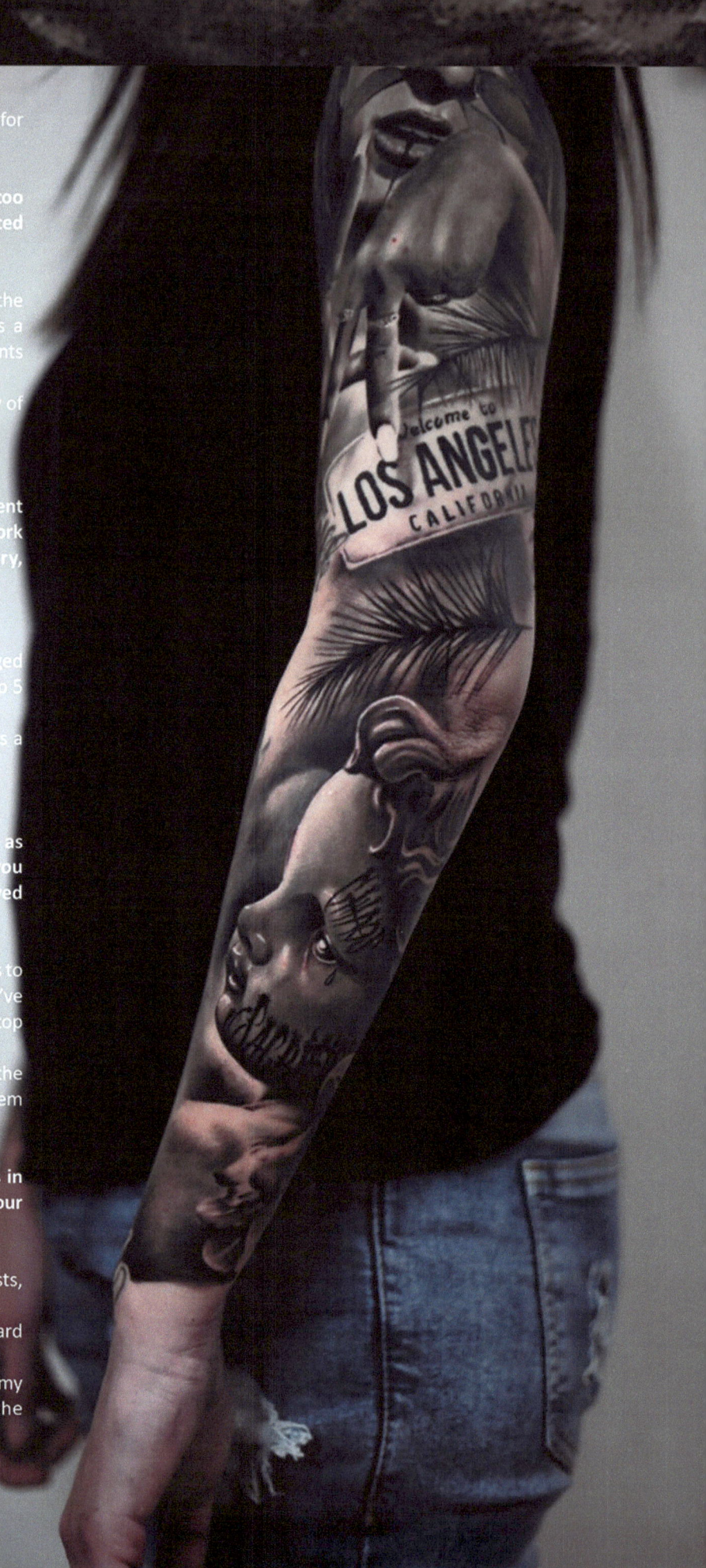

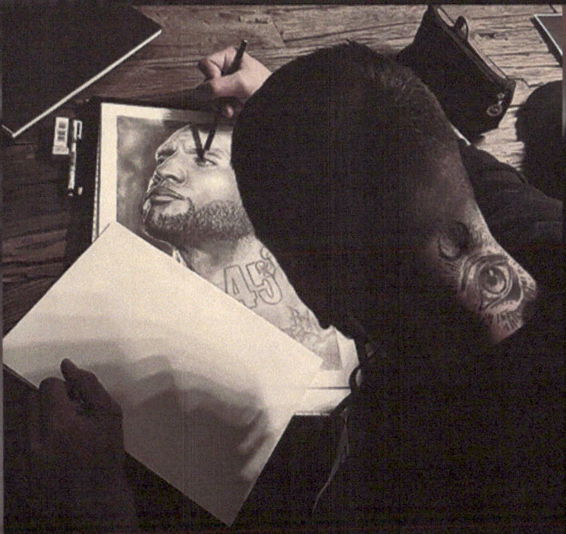

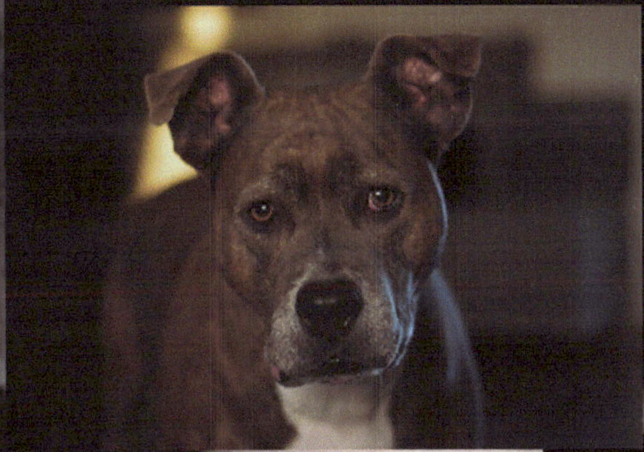

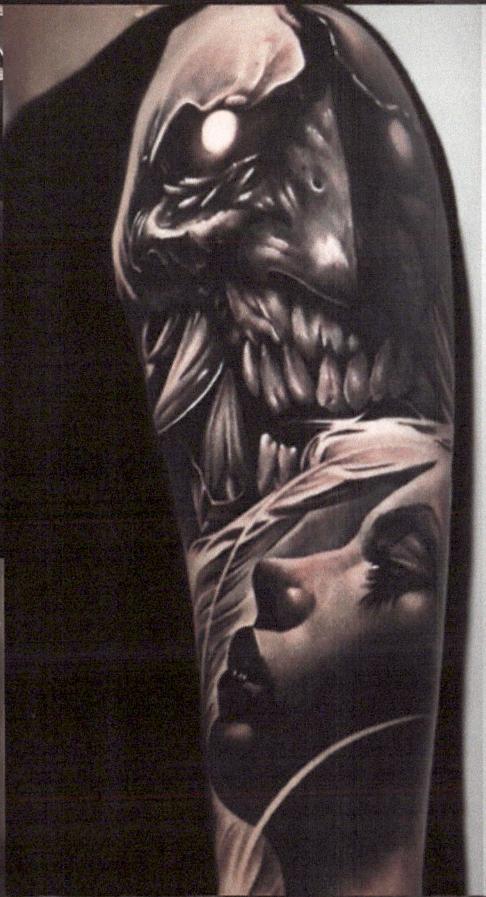

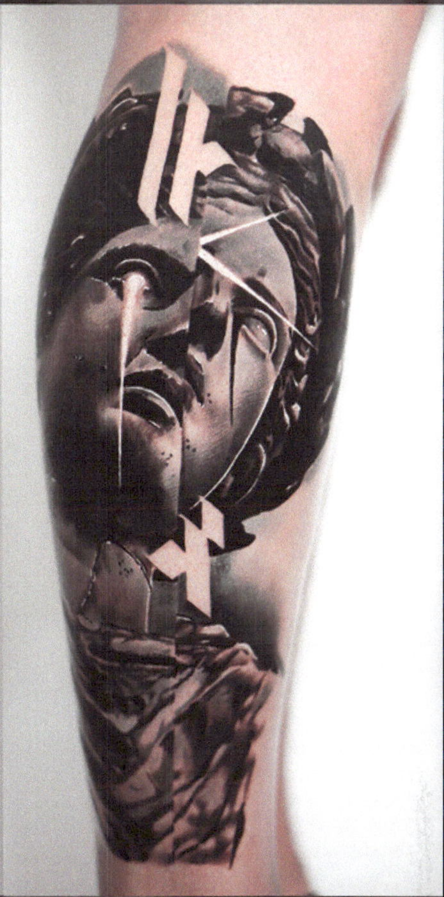

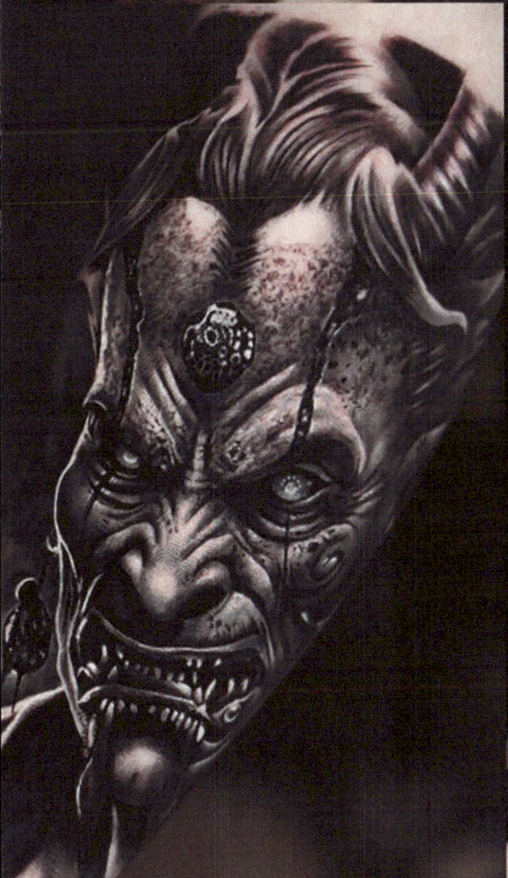

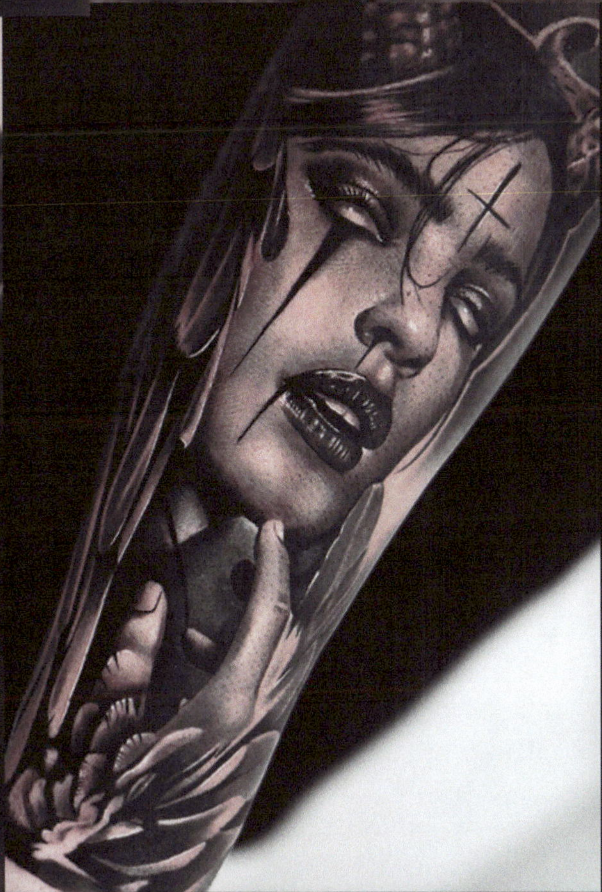

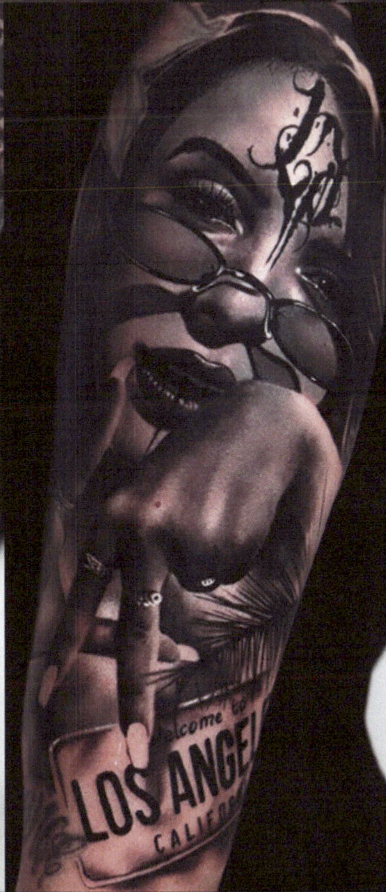

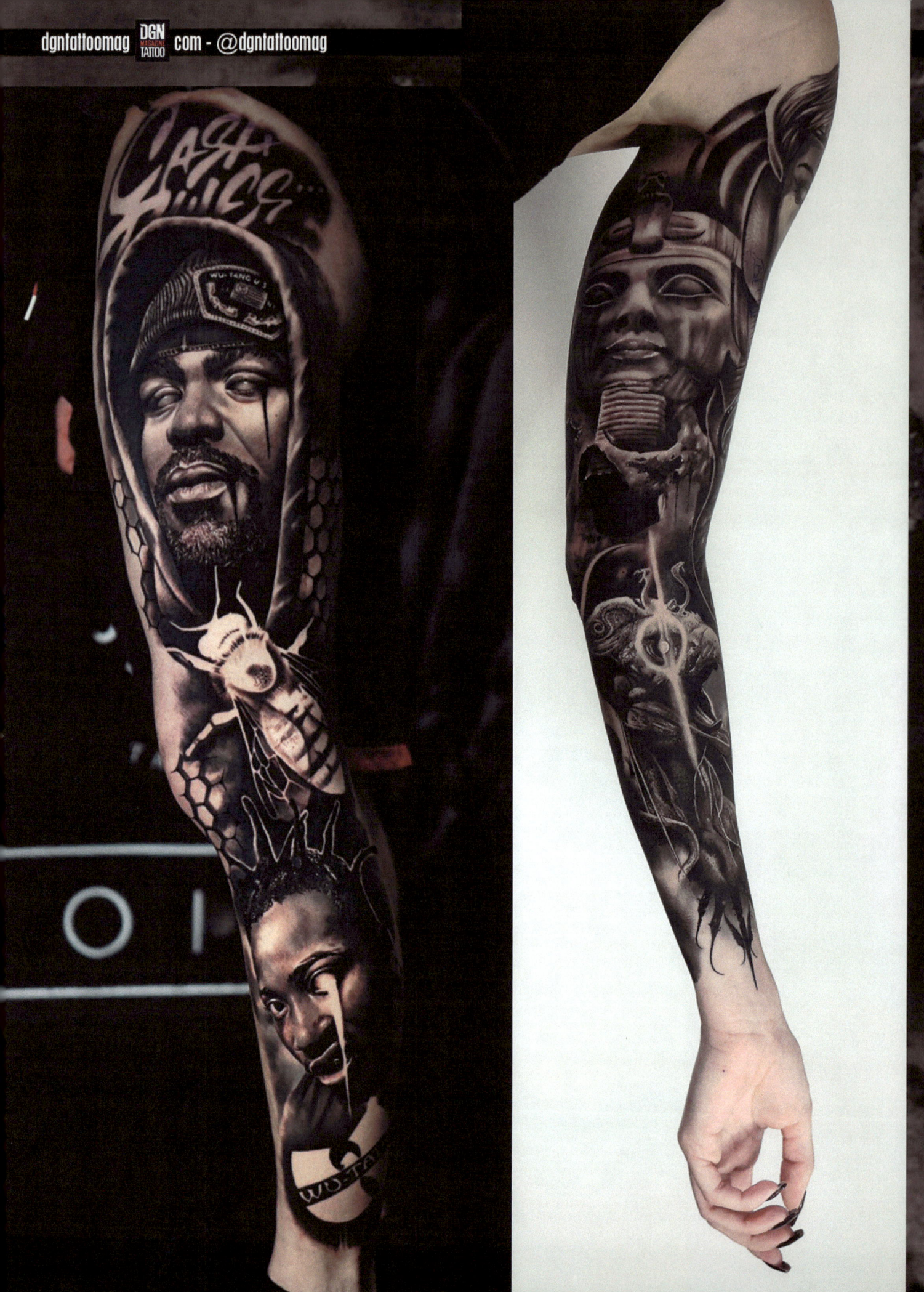

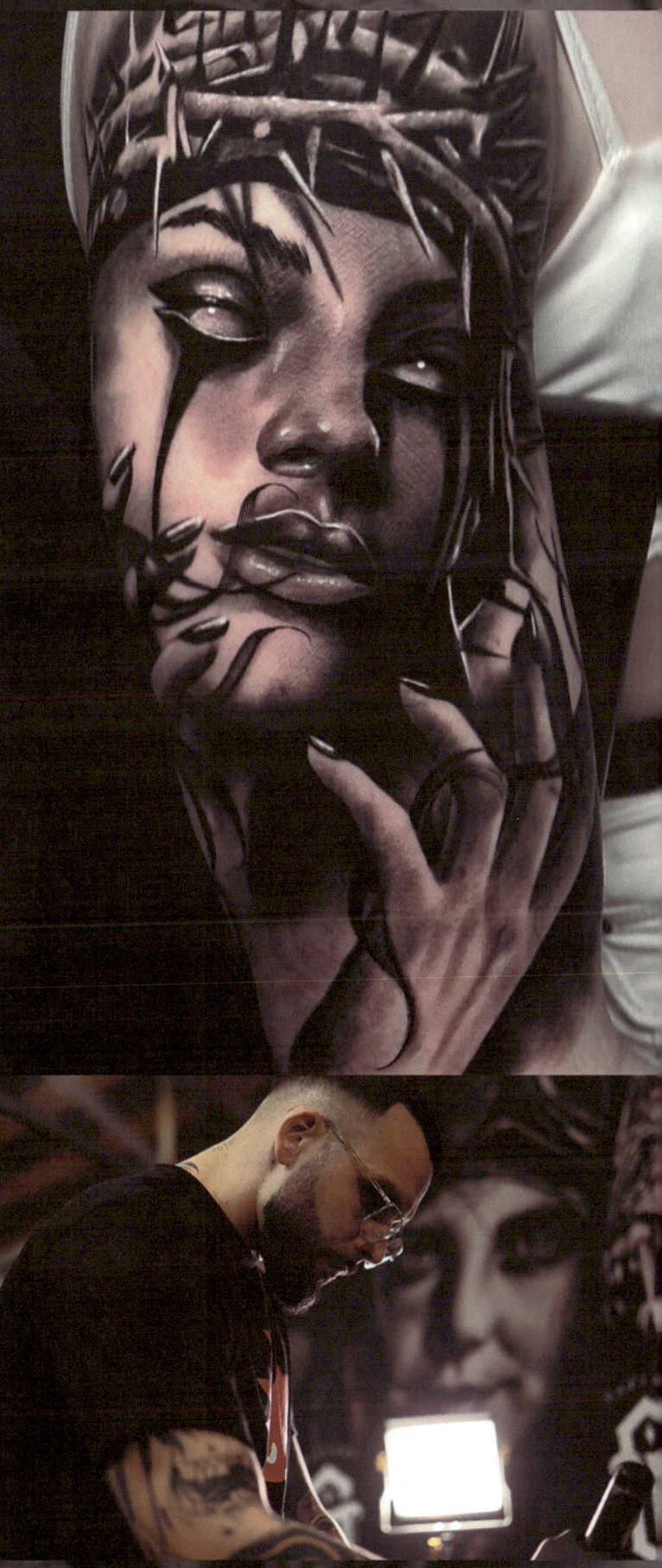

I work a lot on this, I want my artworks to be visible and understandable at the first look, and from far.
My clients are always telling me that they are stopped in the streets, asked where they did their tattoos.
It prove that the first look is Important, I never neglect little details too, of course.

12. Now that you've been recognized as one of the top artists in this international competition among 130 tattoo artists from around the world, how do you think this will impact your career and your focus as a tattoo artist in the future?

My implication stays the same since years, I like the challenge that this work imposes, in a very cerebral way.
There's a lot of parameters to make a good tattoo.
I hope that my clients and future clients will be glad of this ranking at DGN.
For the moment I keep a cool head and I continue my quest of perfection.

13.Is there a message or expression of gratitude you'd like to convey to the jury and your followers for this achievement?

Of course ! First of all I want to thank the judges ! They are so remarkable ! I'm so glad to have the chance to show them my work.
And I want to thank the followers too, they support me and my work daily, thank you all for your trust.

14. What are your future goals as a tattoo artist?Do you have any projects or styles you'd like to explore in the future?

I want to open a dope and big studio with my team ! The best shop in south of France, with big spaces, great lights, where the clients would live the best tattoo experience of their life.
I want to continue to take part to contests too, the most known, in order to be recognized as an unavoidable name in the tattoo world.
For the style I will stay in realism, perfect my style and my graphic codes.
Gaining fame thanks to the singularity of my creations.

15.If someone wishes to contact you to schedule an appointment or learn more about your work, what is the best way to do so?

I've created my own site online :www.gaetano-tattoo.com
The client can send me all the inspirations he/she has.
It's the best way for me to treat the requests.

The passion for art often emerges in childhood, a seed that grows and flourishes over the years. For Colombian tattoo artist David Giraldo

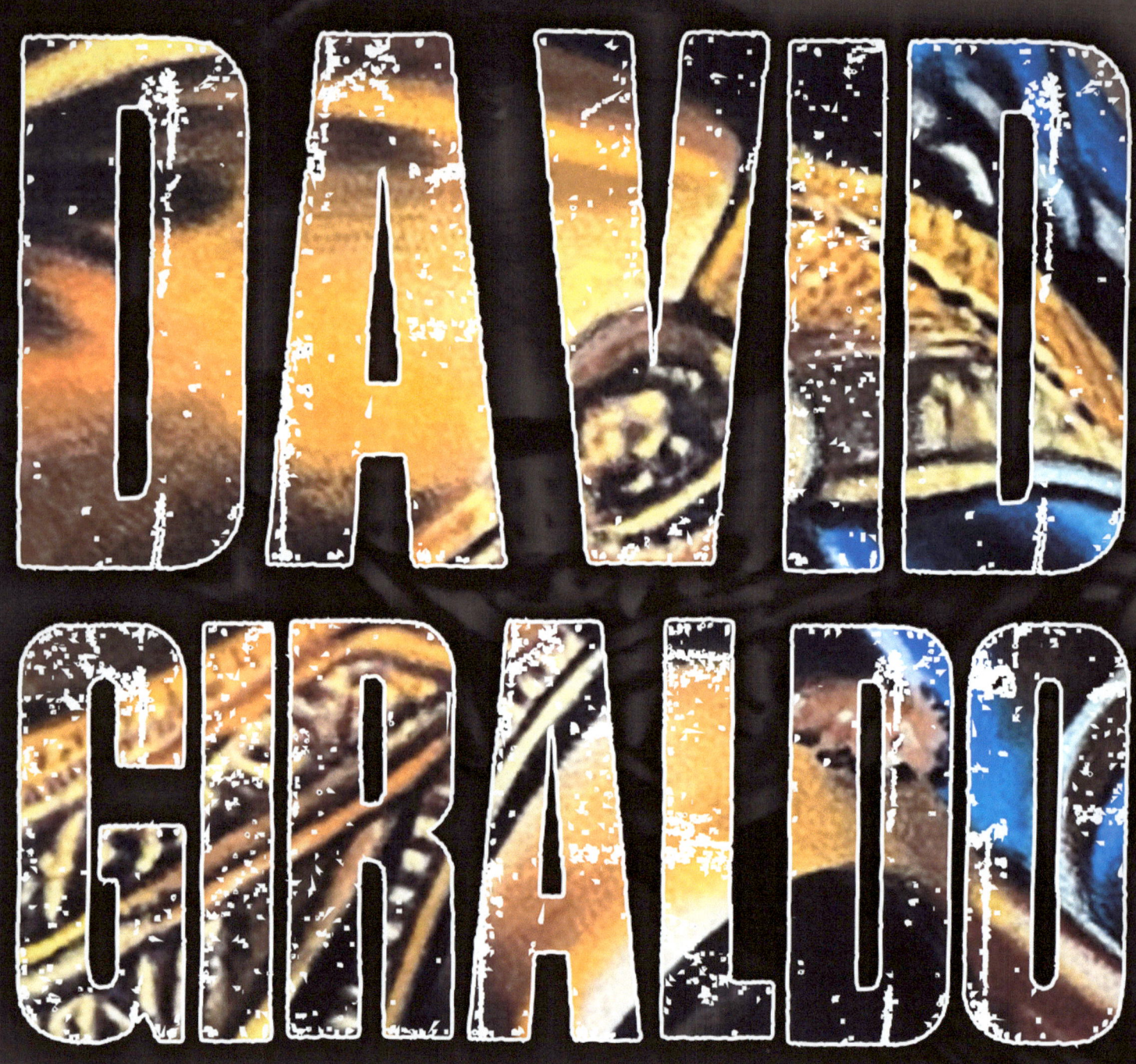

DAVID GIRALDO

A Tattooed Triumph in the Hearts of the Public and the Jury of Excellence

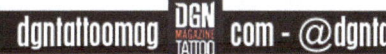

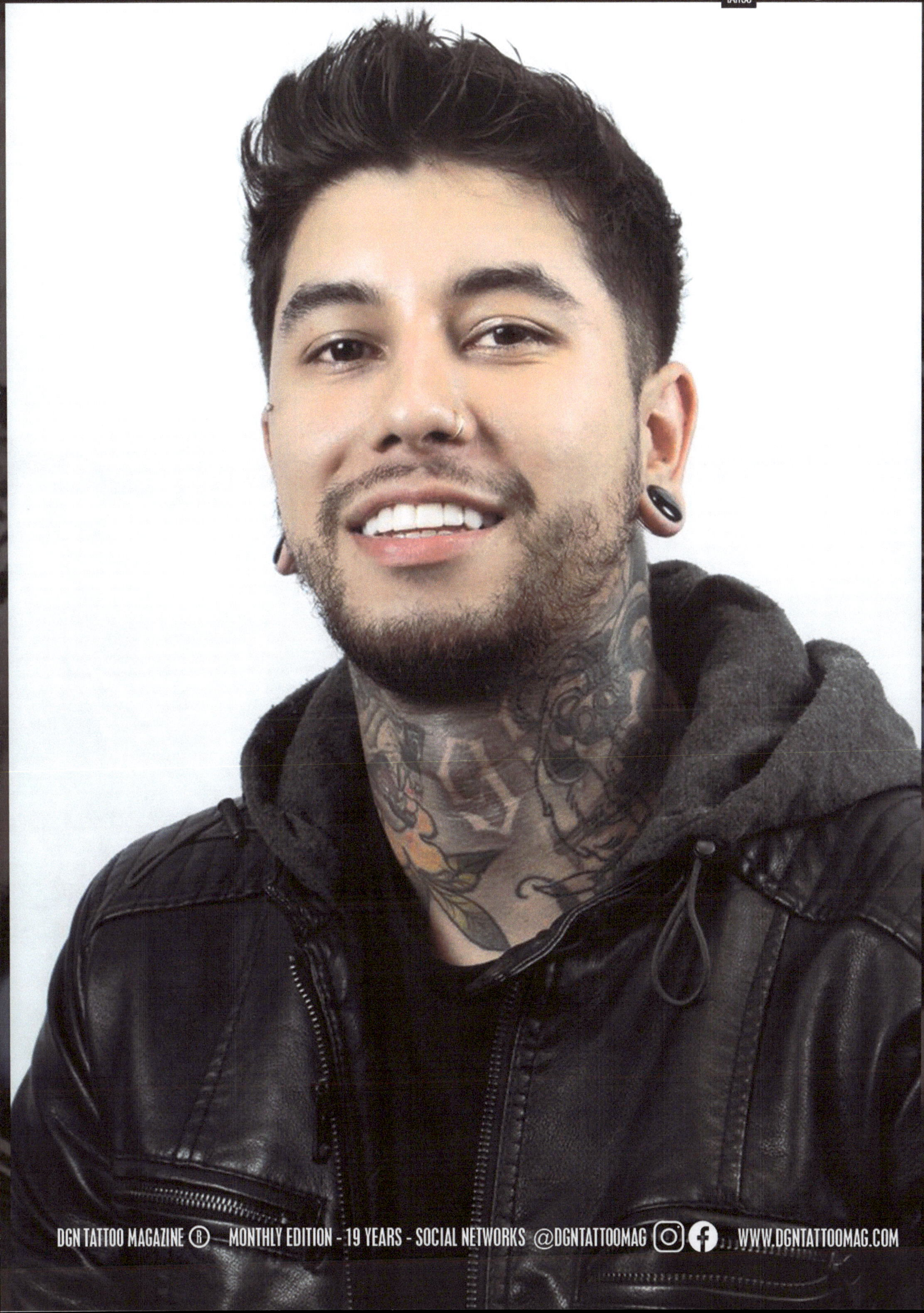

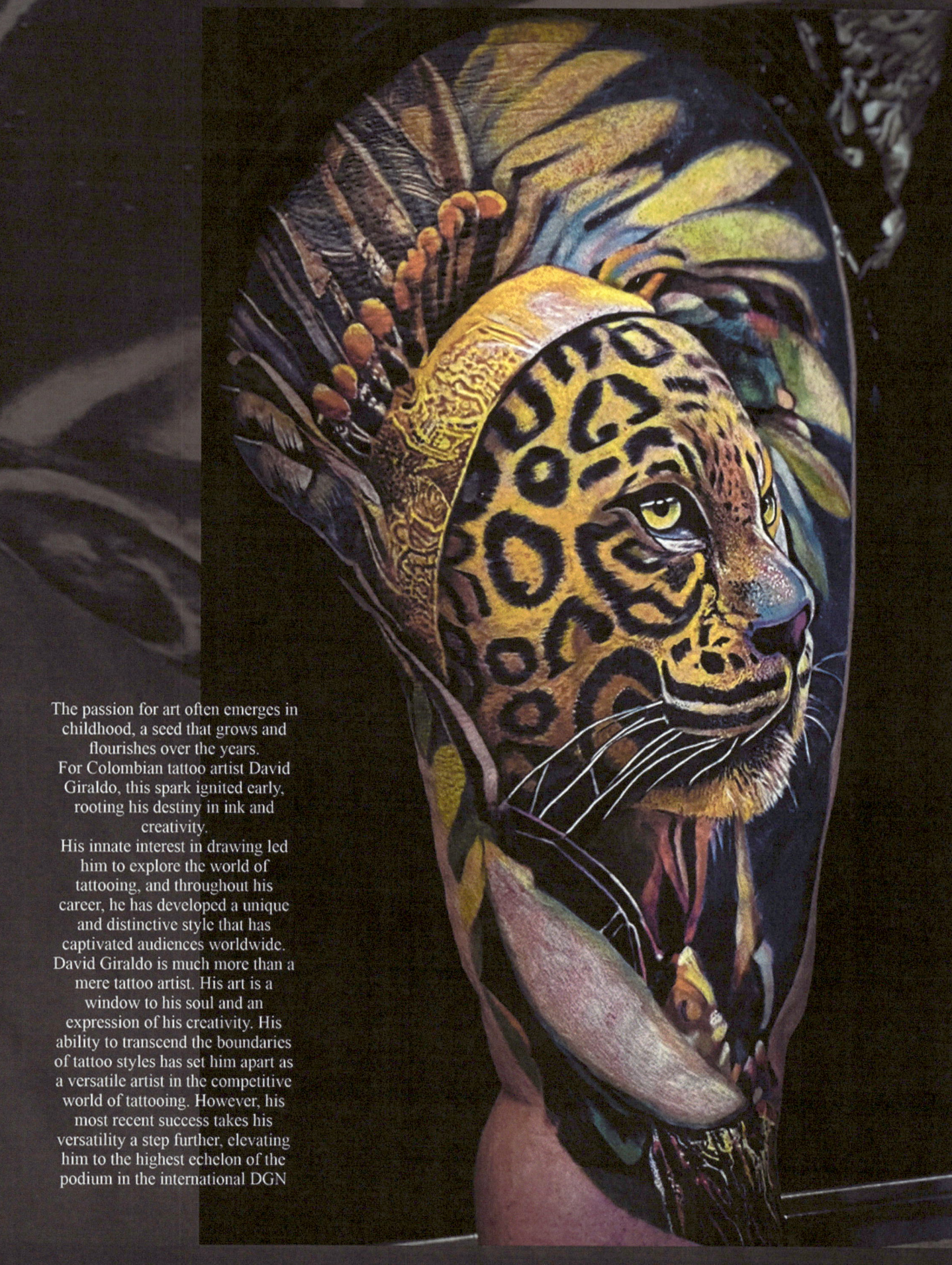

The passion for art often emerges in childhood, a seed that grows and flourishes over the years. For Colombian tattoo artist David Giraldo, this spark ignited early, rooting his destiny in ink and creativity.

His innate interest in drawing led him to explore the world of tattooing, and throughout his career, he has developed a unique and distinctive style that has captivated audiences worldwide. David Giraldo is much more than a mere tattoo artist. His art is a window to his soul and an expression of his creativity. His ability to transcend the boundaries of tattoo styles has set him apart as a versatile artist in the competitive world of tattooing. However, his most recent success takes his versatility a step further, elevating him to the highest echelon of the podium in the international DGN

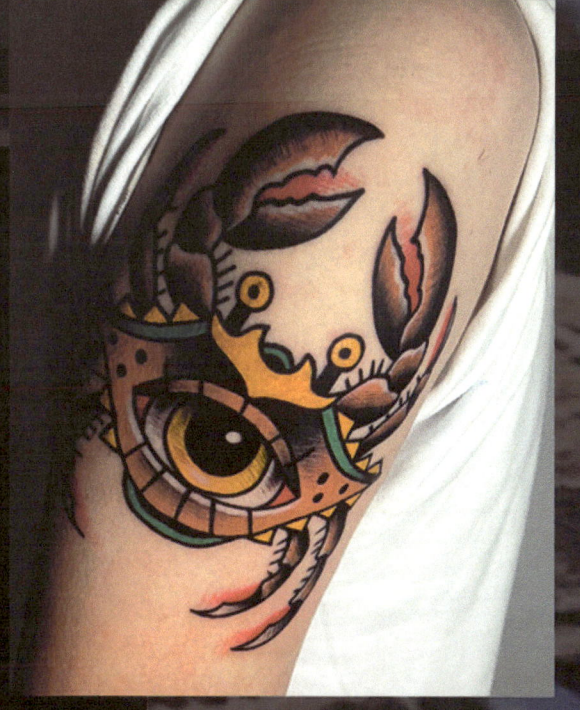

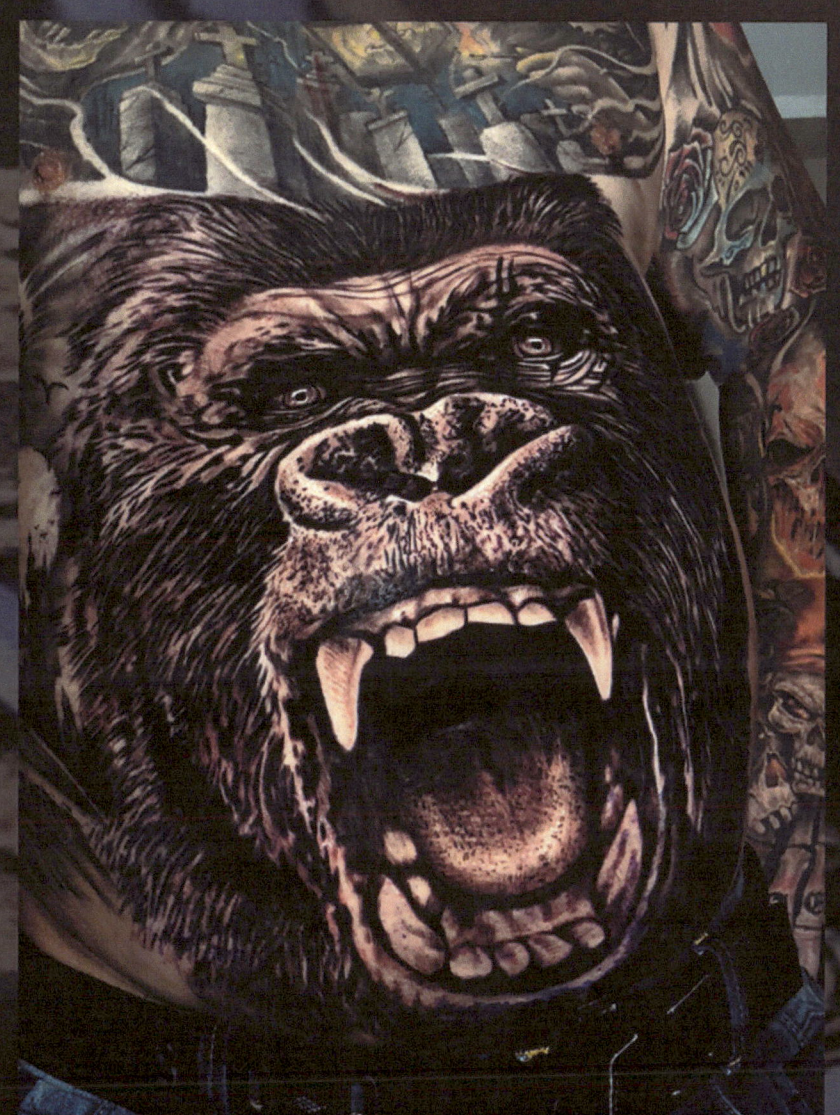

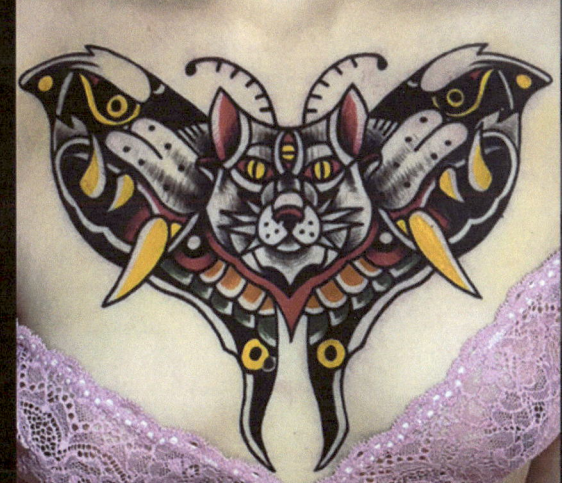

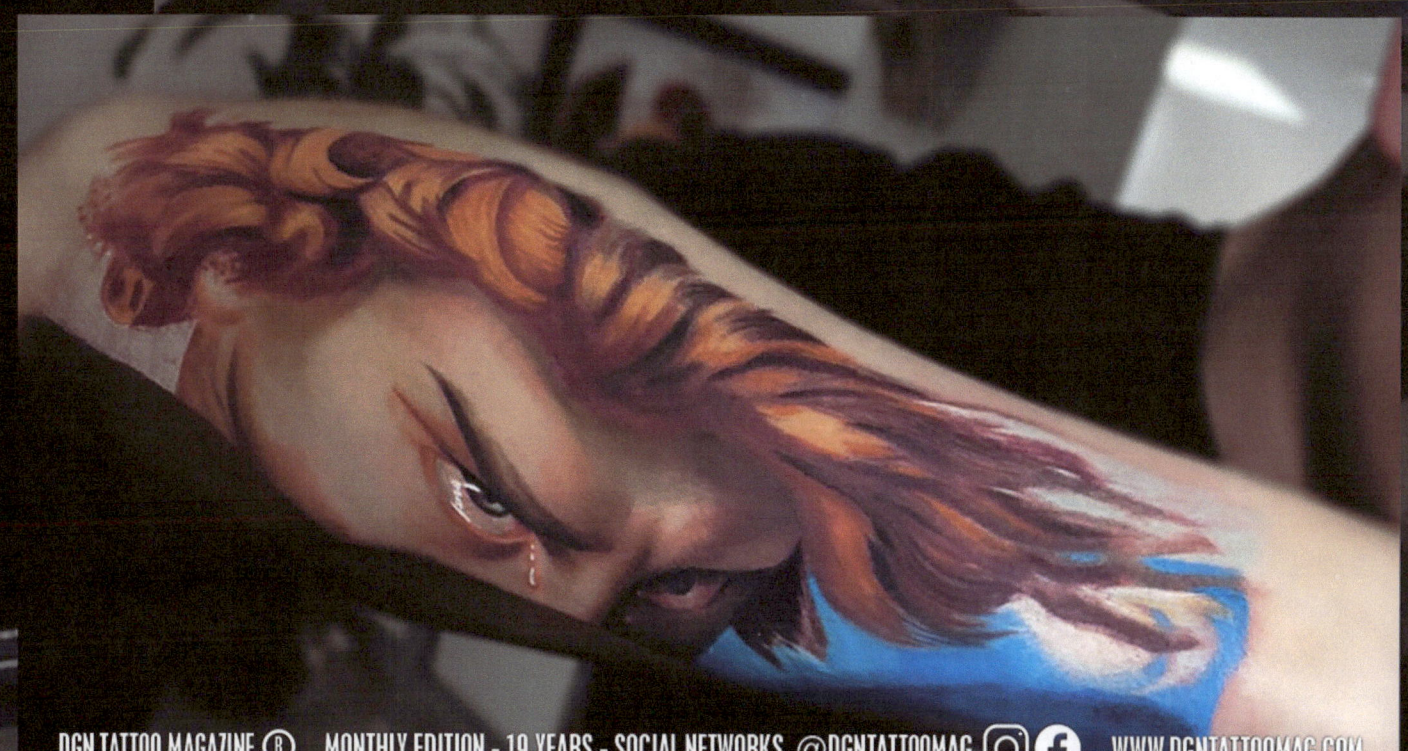

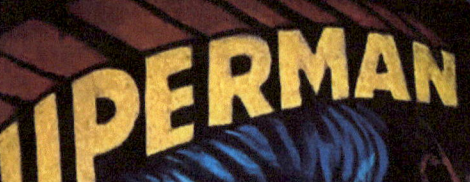

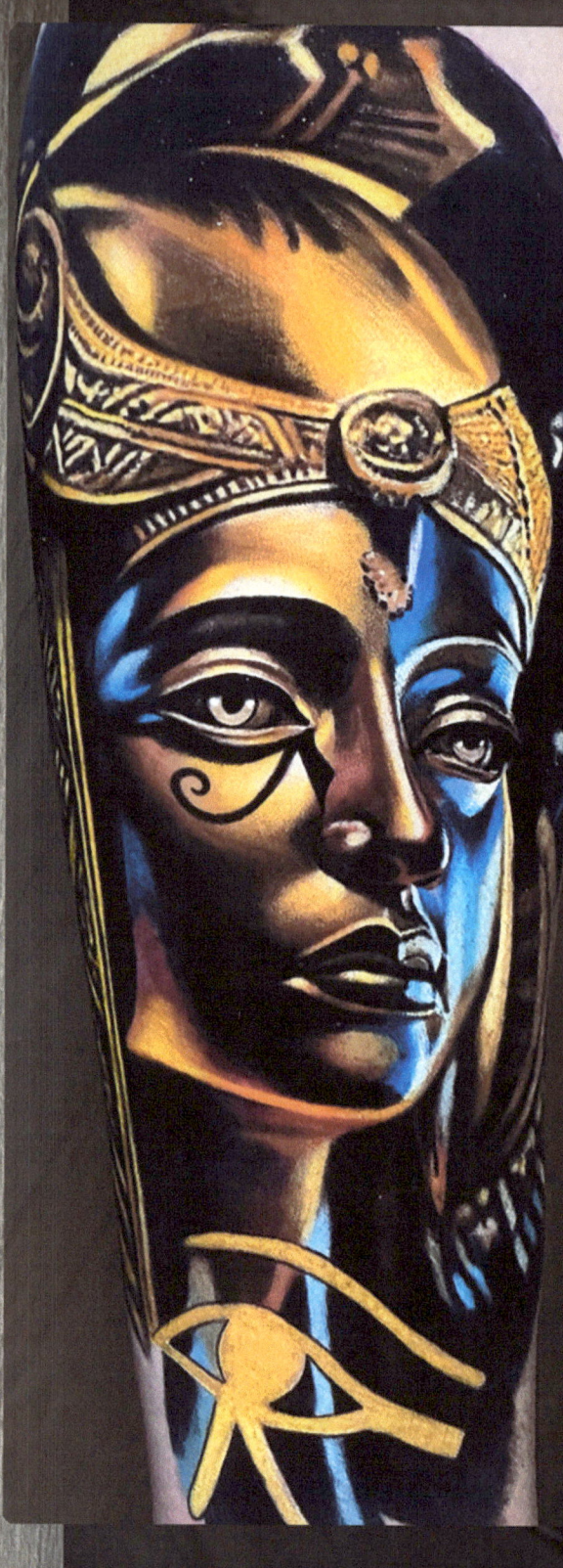

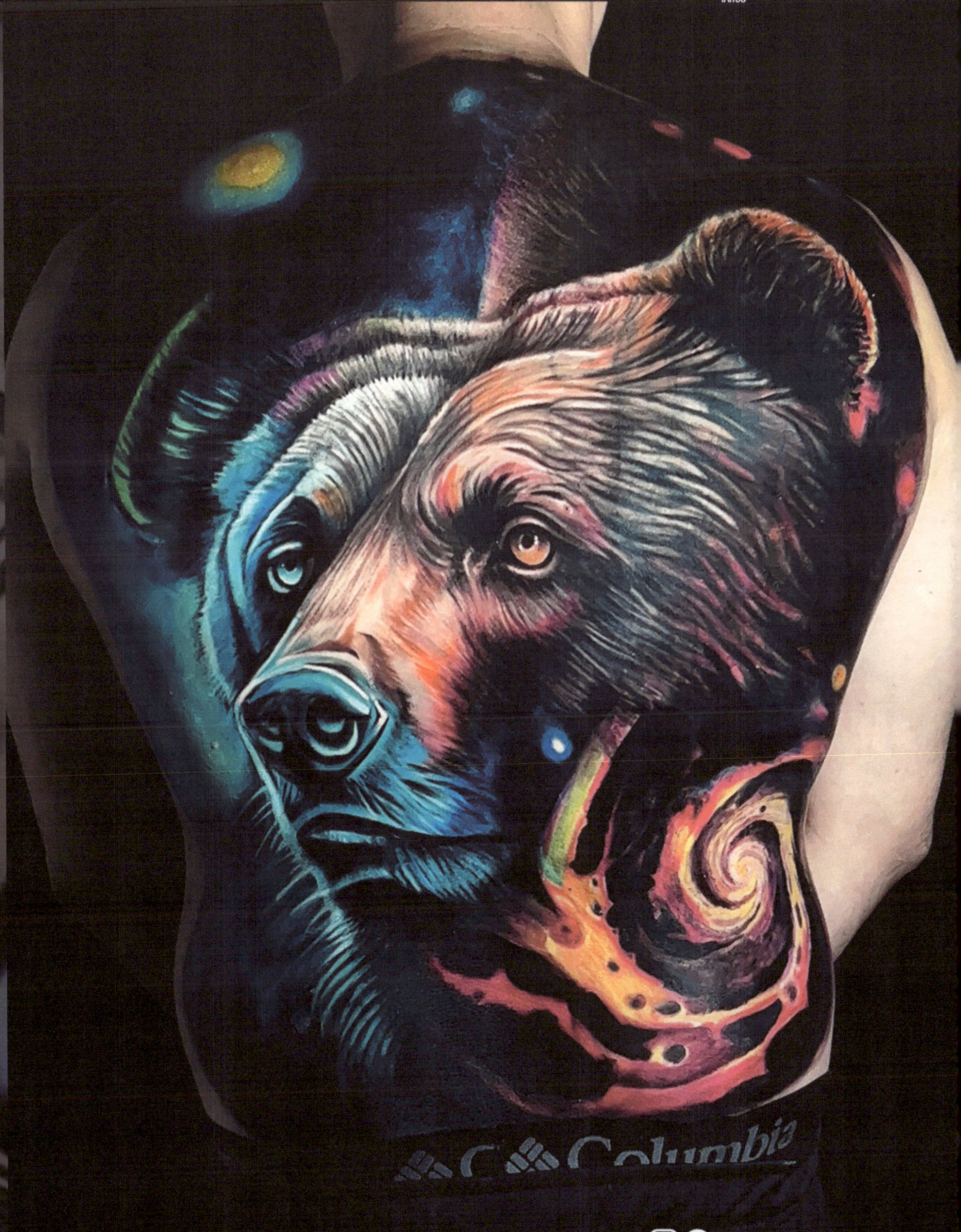
Columbia

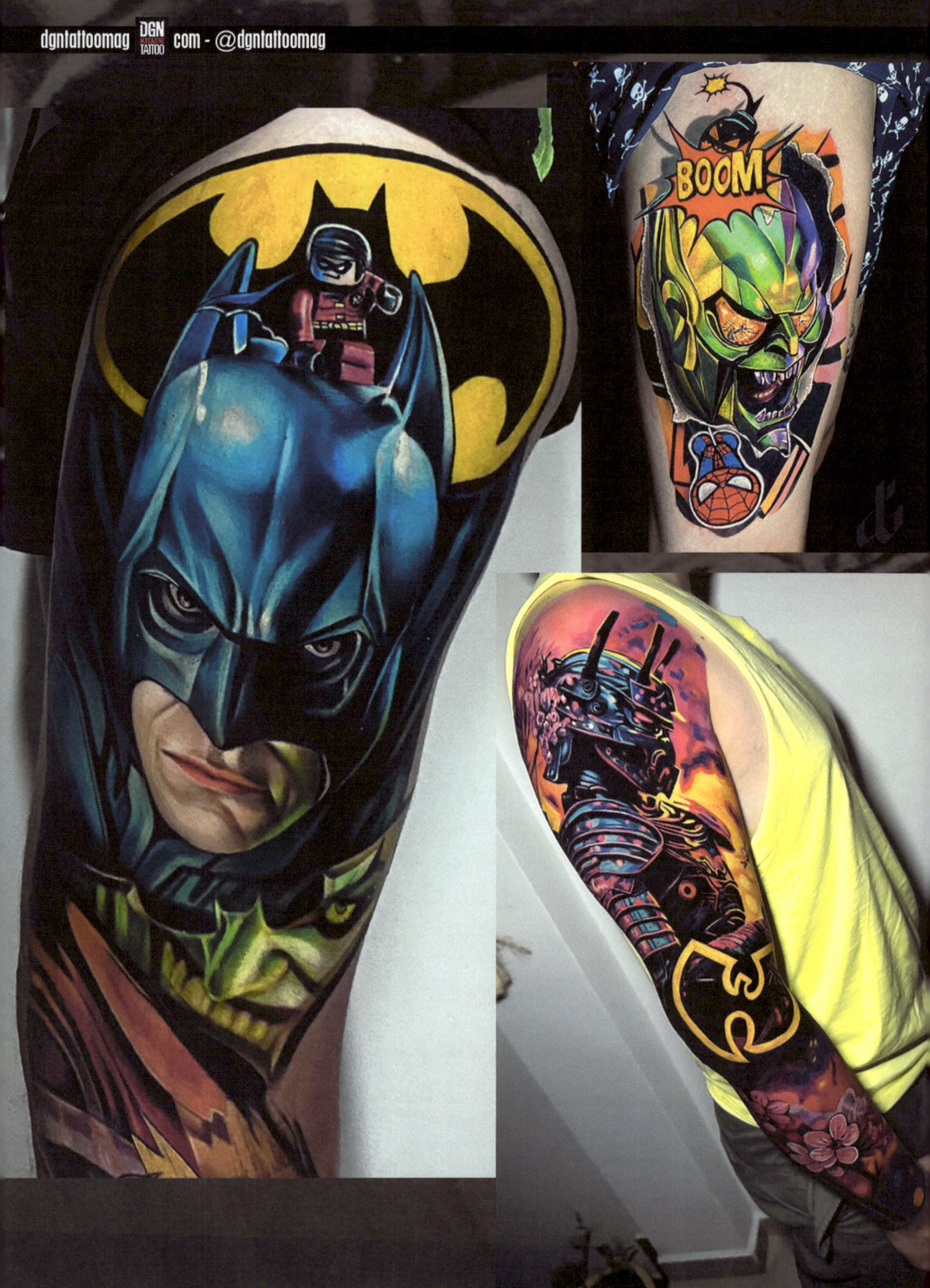

Tattoo Magazine competition. This competition is a true battleground for tattoo artists. With a jury of excellence and the highest caliber, composed of Victor Portugal, Myke Chambers, Dave Paulo, Valentina Riabova, Andrei Stepanov, and Haewall, it is not an achievement to be taken lightly. Recognition from these experts is bestowed only upon those who have demonstrated exceptional talent in the art of tattooing.

But what sets David Giraldo apart is his double triumph in the competition. He was chosen by the public, an accomplishment that reveals the immense affection his audience holds for him. This is not only an achievement in his career but also a testament to the strong bond he has forged with his followers. Tattooing, as an art form, is often a deeply personal experience, and David has managed to touch the hearts of those who wear his art on their skin.

Winning in the versatile category in a competition of this magnitude is a testament to his ability to tackle any tattoo style with skill and mastery. From realism to Oriental, from black and white tattoos to the most colorful, David Giraldo has proven to be a true chameleon in the world of tattooing.

The story of David Giraldo serves as a reminder that passion, talent, and dedication can lead to remarkable achievements. His art not only adorns the skin of his clients but also tells the story of his own artistic evolution. In this triumph in the international DGN Tattoo Magazine competition, the radiance of a tattoo artist who has achieved the status of a star in the tattooing firmament is reflected.

David Giraldo is a name we will continue to hear, admire, and carry on our skin in the years to come. His versatility and ability to conquer both the public and the jury of excellence have propelled him to the pinnacle of the art of tattooing. With his talent and charisma, this Colombian tattoo artist is destined to leave an indelible mark on the global tattooing community.

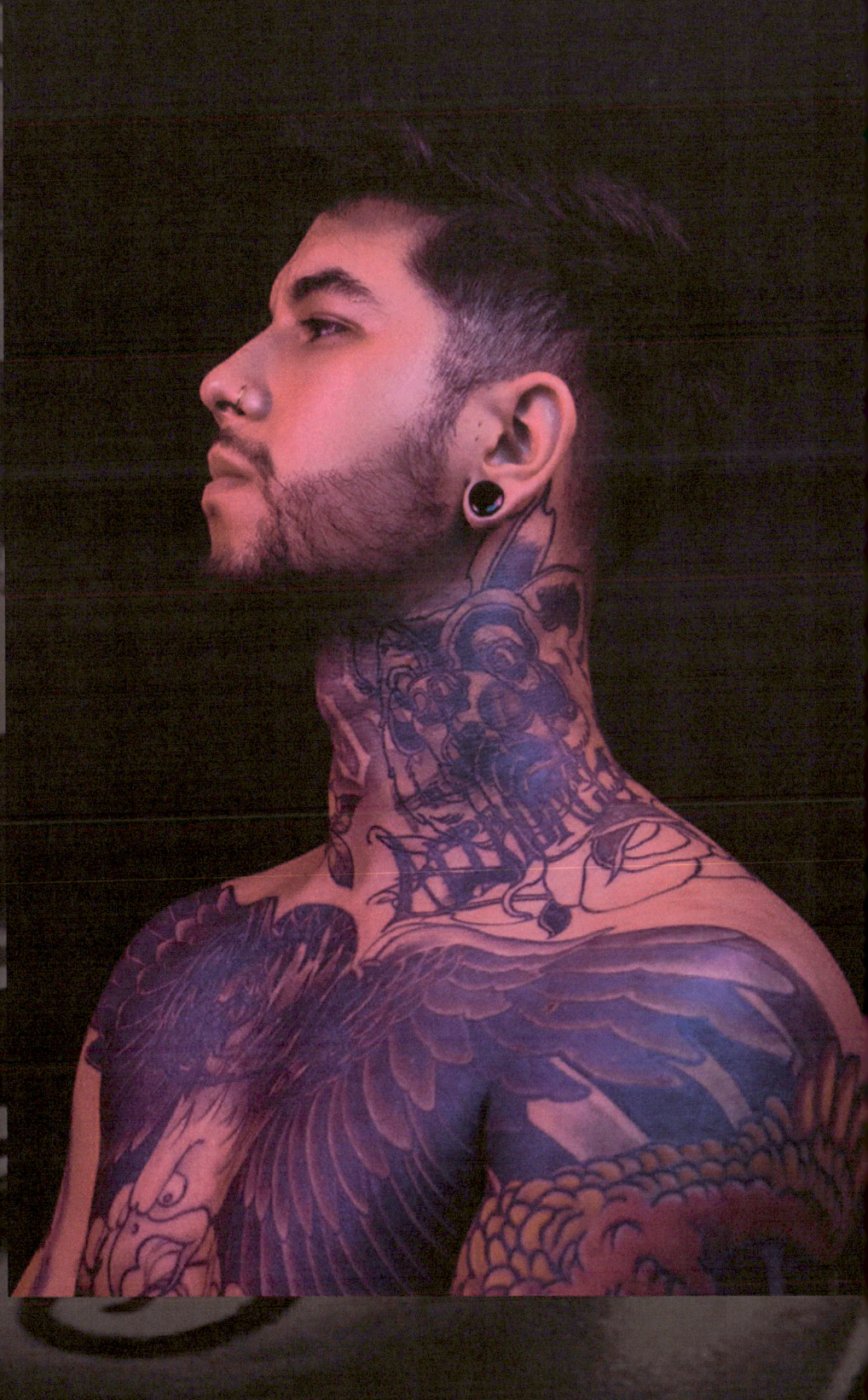

Frankfurt / Germany - @nofuckingidols - +49 17670611745

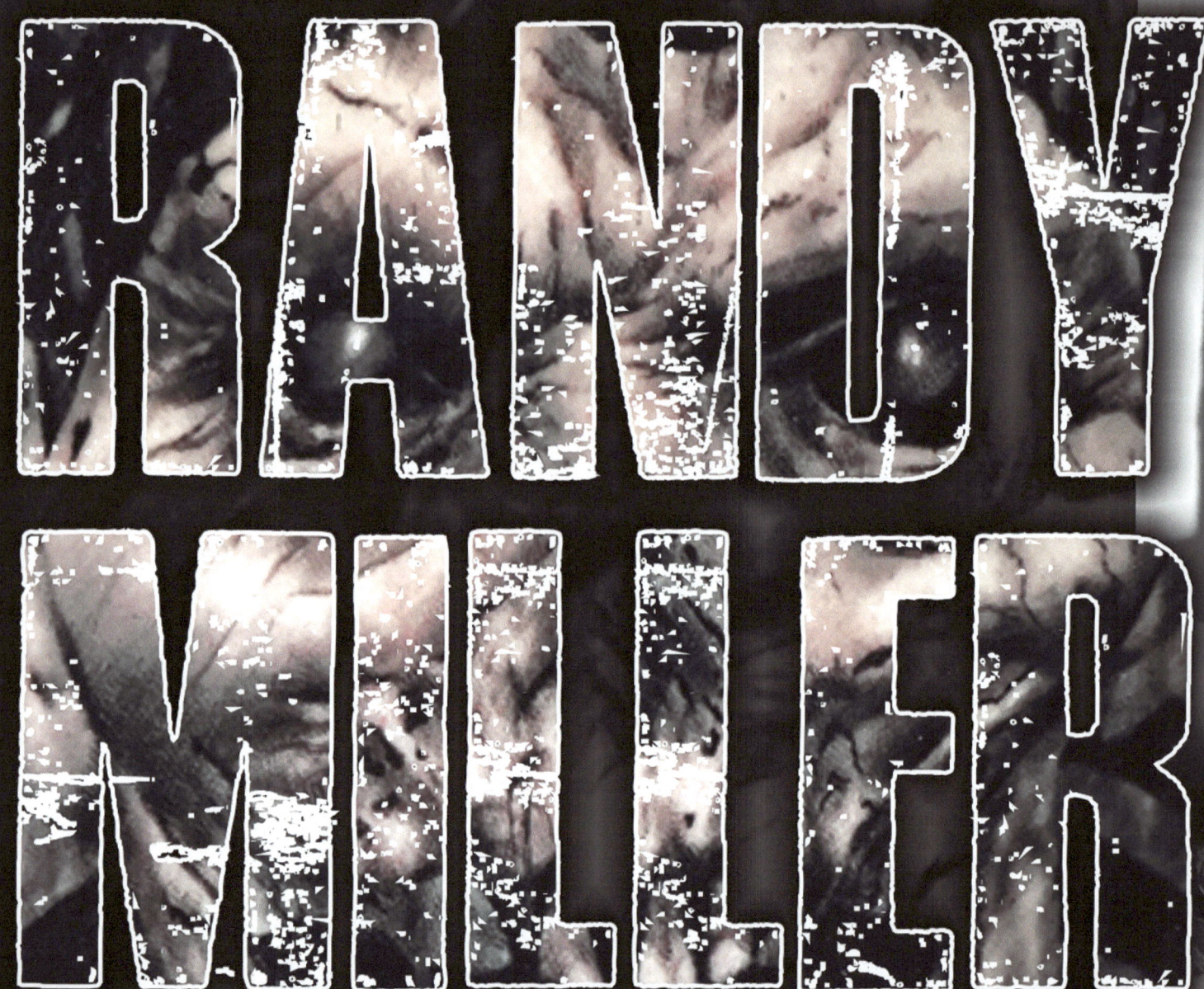

RANDY MILLER

Meet Randy Miller, a talented tattoo artist specializing in realistic tattoos, particularly in the black and grey style. His journey began six years ago, driven by a passion for lifelike artistry. Randy's dedication to capturing intricate details on skin sets him apart. He recently earned recognition as one of the top 5 tattoo artists in DGN Tattoo Magazine's contest, further inspiring his commitment to artistic expression through tattooing.

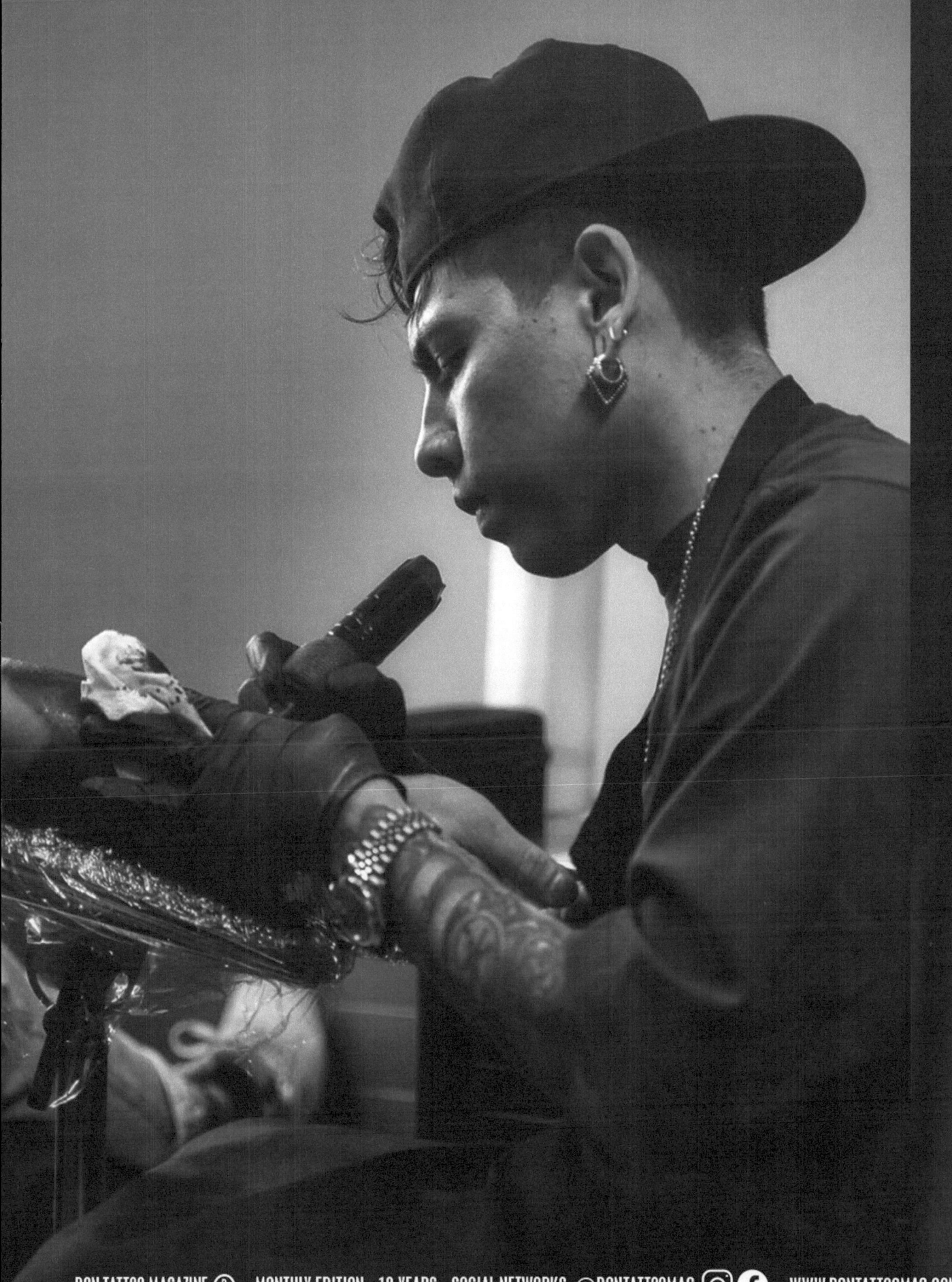

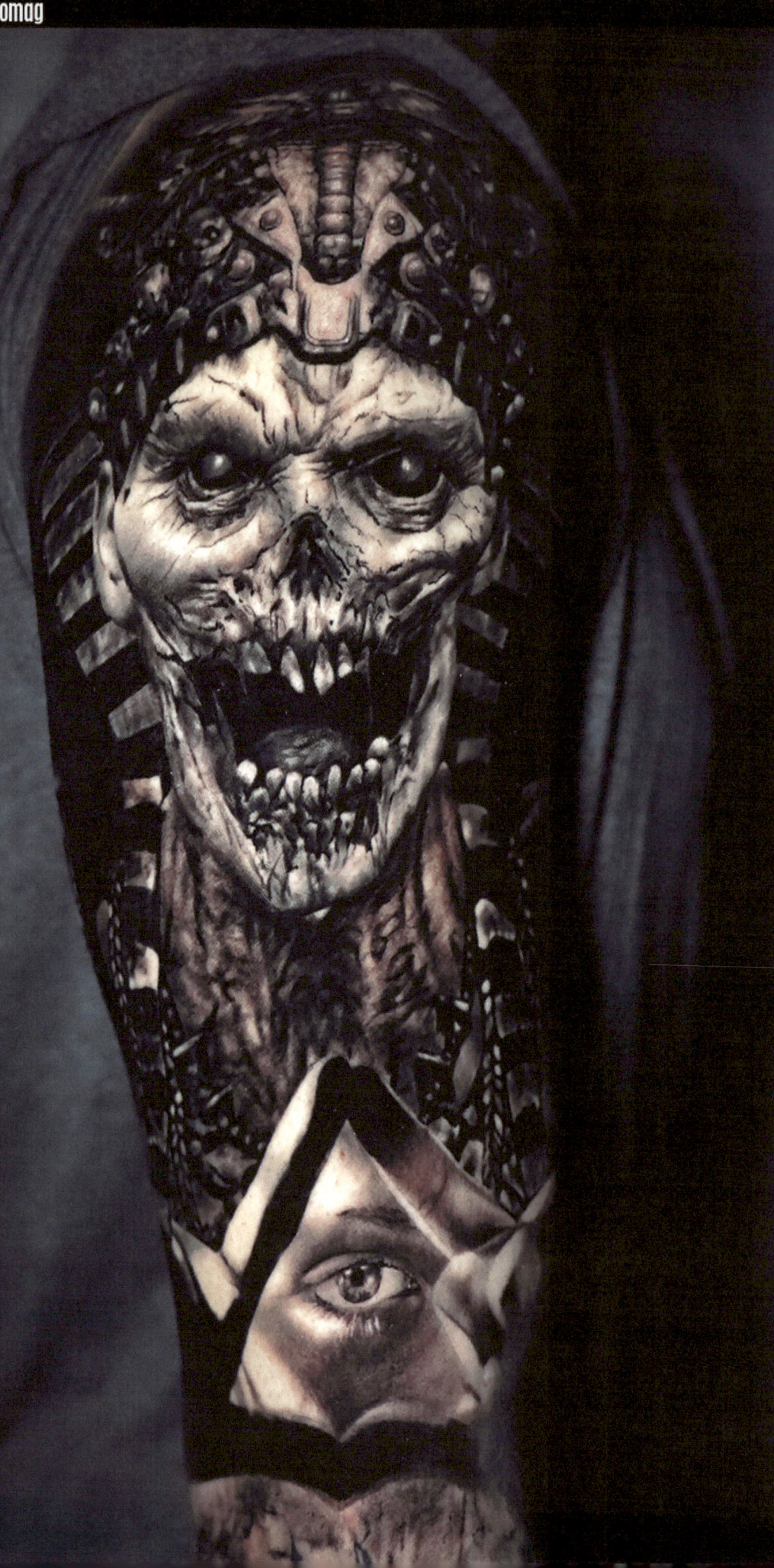

Hey there, I'm Randy Miller, My journey as a tattoo artist began about 6 years ago. I was always captivated by the intricate details and lifelike quality of realistic art. I spent years refining my skills, and studying human anatomy to truly capture the essence of realism in my tattoo.

The black and grey style just resonates with me on a different level. It's like sculpting with shadows and light to create depth and emotion. When it comes to realistic tattoos, the joy lies in the challenge of replicating real-life subjects on skin. The satisfaction of seeing a portrait or an intricate piece come together in shades of grey is beyond words.

The process starts with a thorough consultation. I want to understand not only the subject matter but also the emotional connection my client has with it. Then comes the research phase, where I gather reference images and study the subject from different angles. From there, I create a custom design that captures all the intricate details and brings the subject to life on the skin. When working on fine details, I make sure to choose a size that allows for proper ink saturation and healing. I also advise my clients

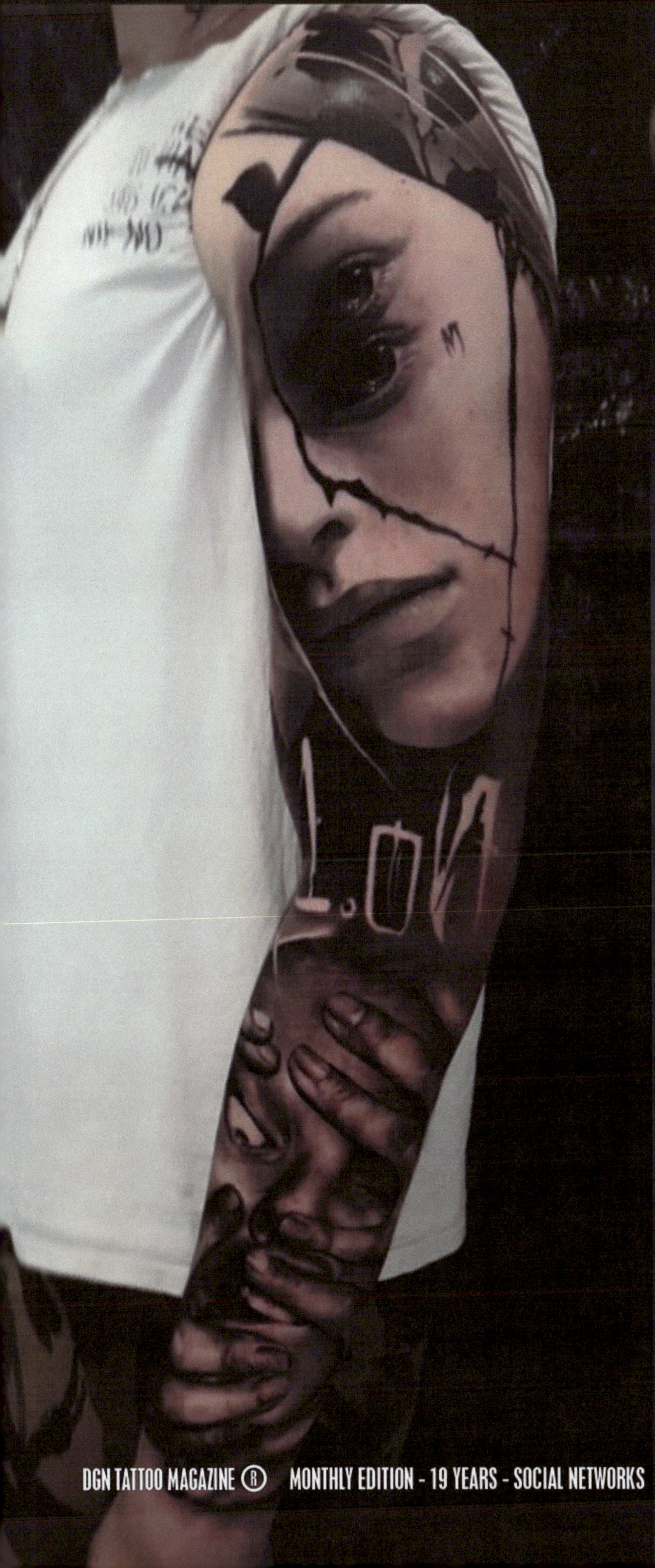

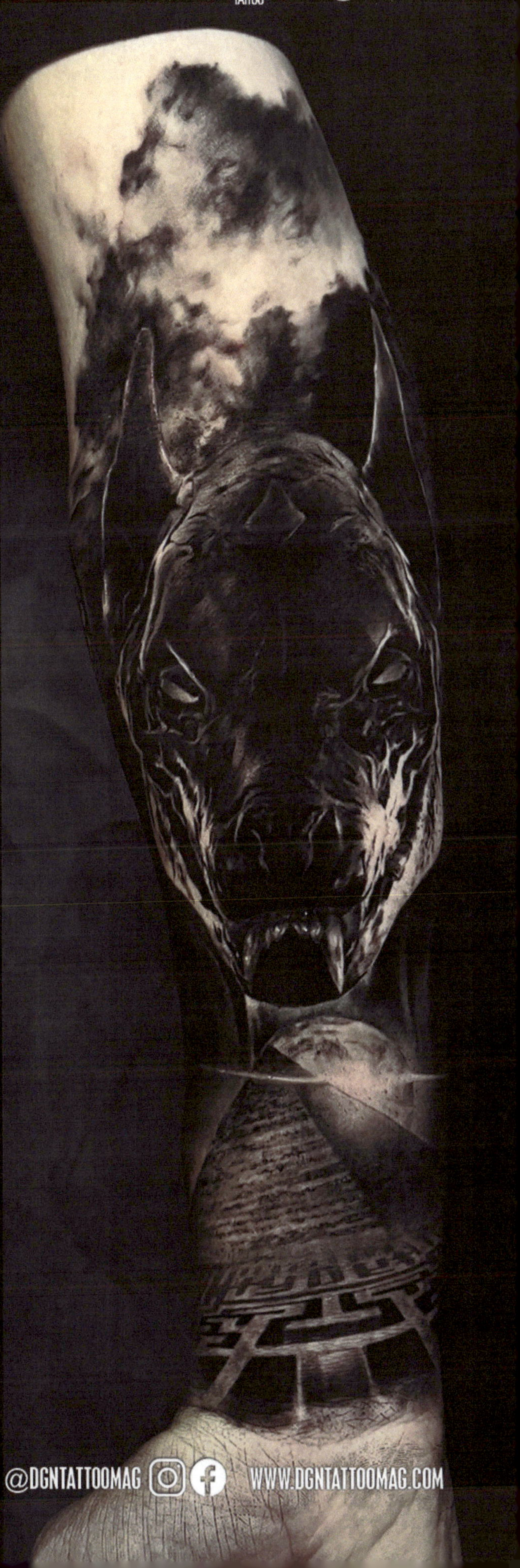

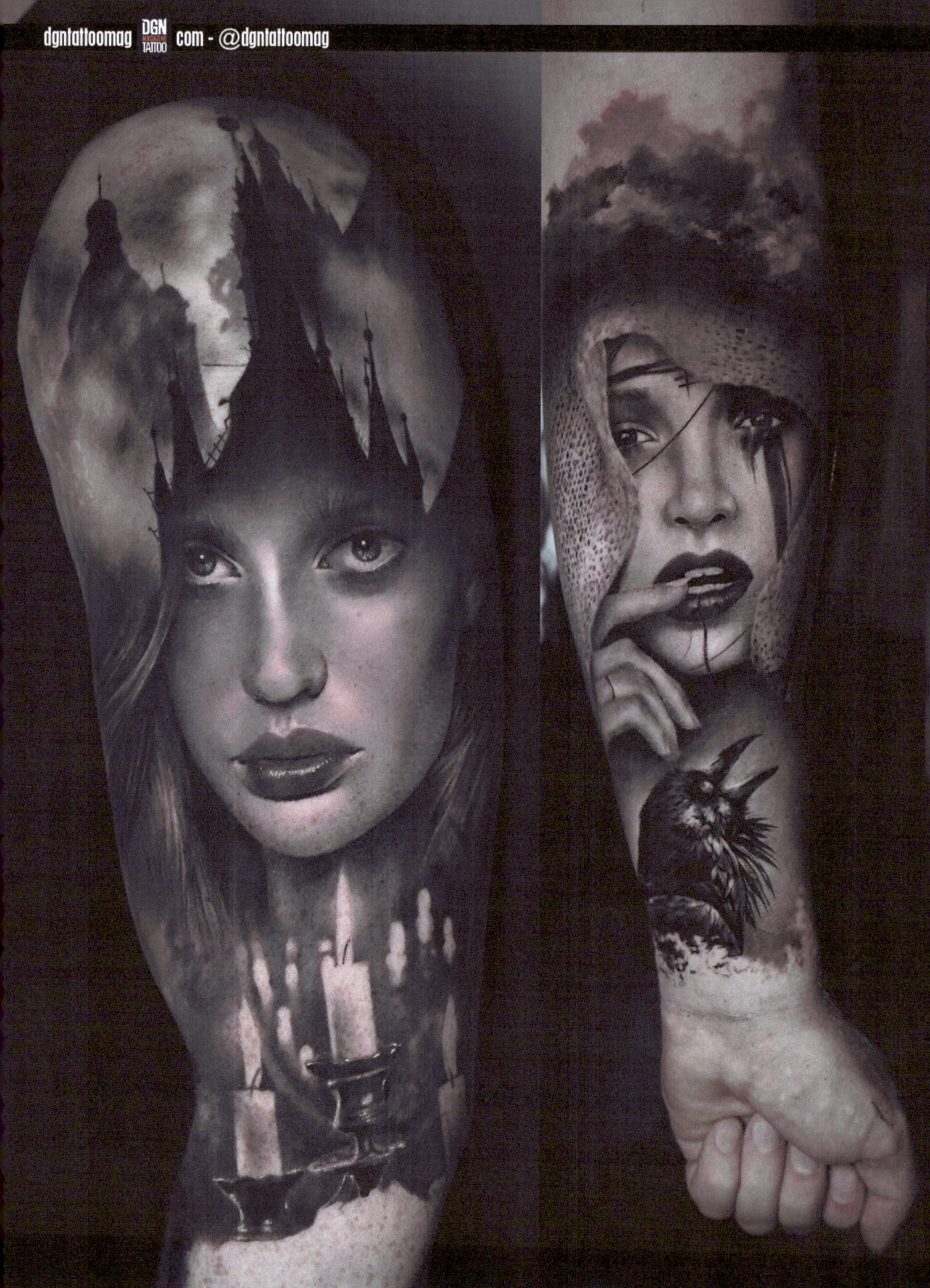

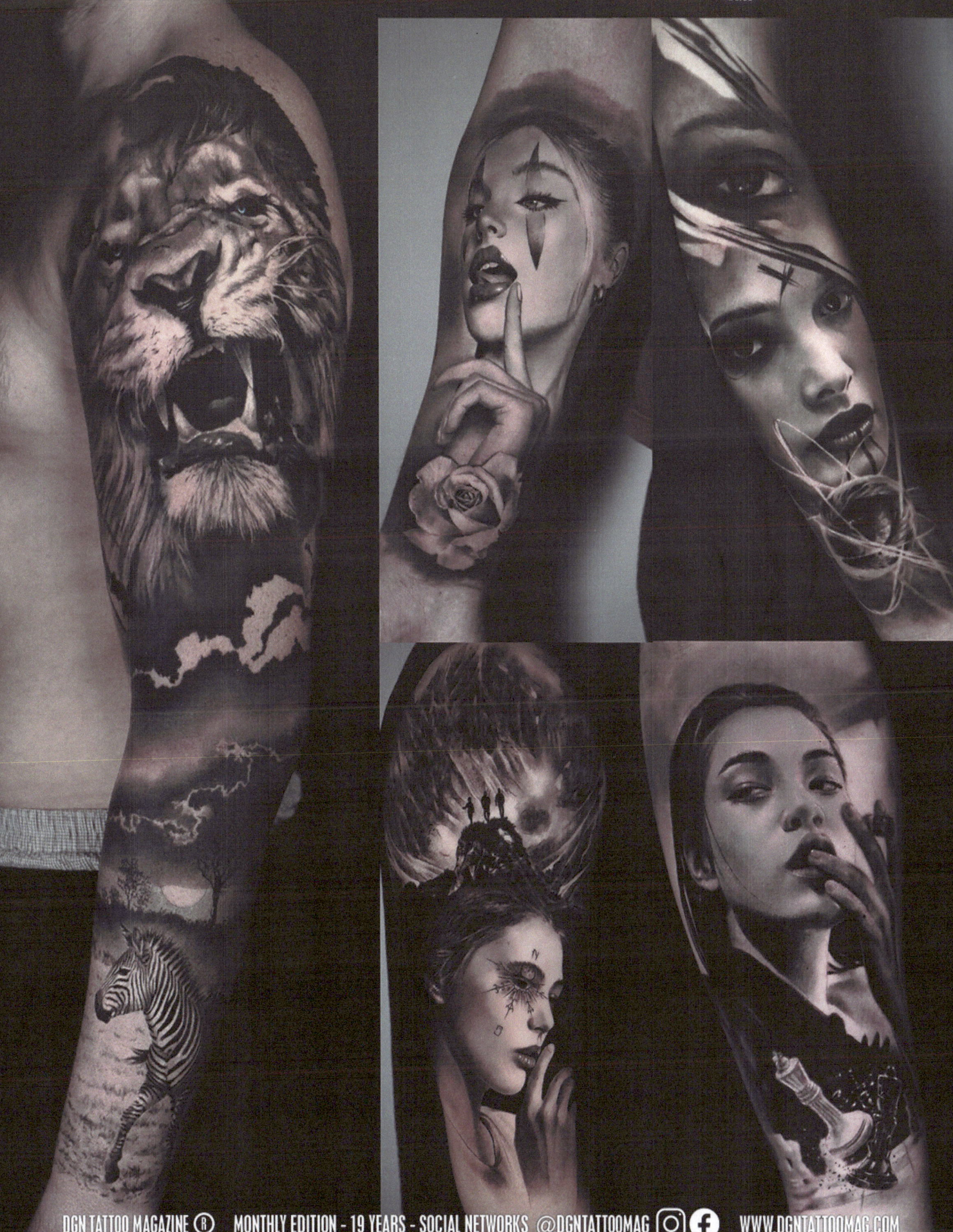

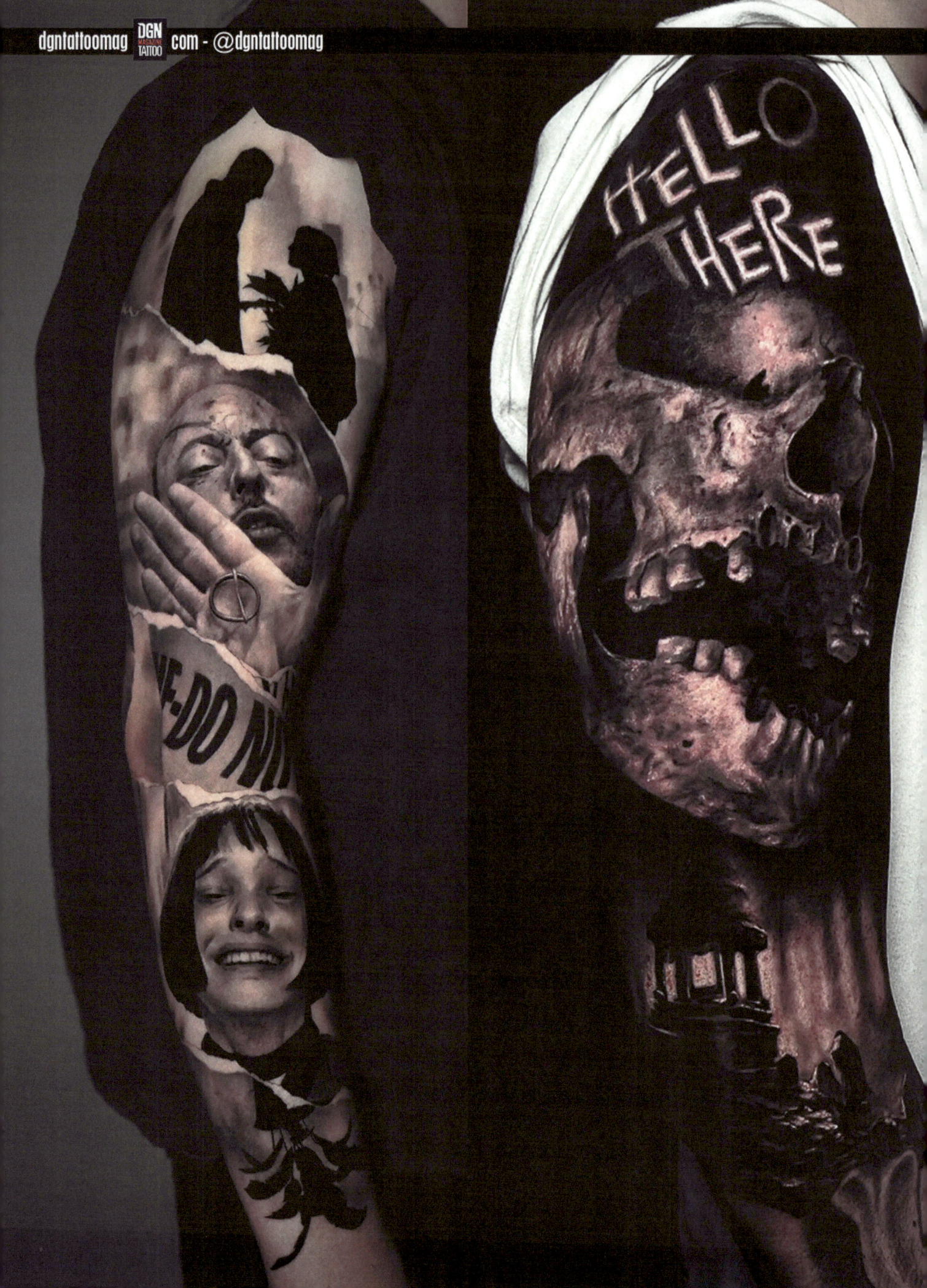

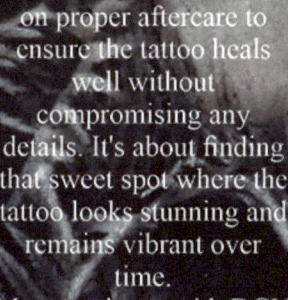

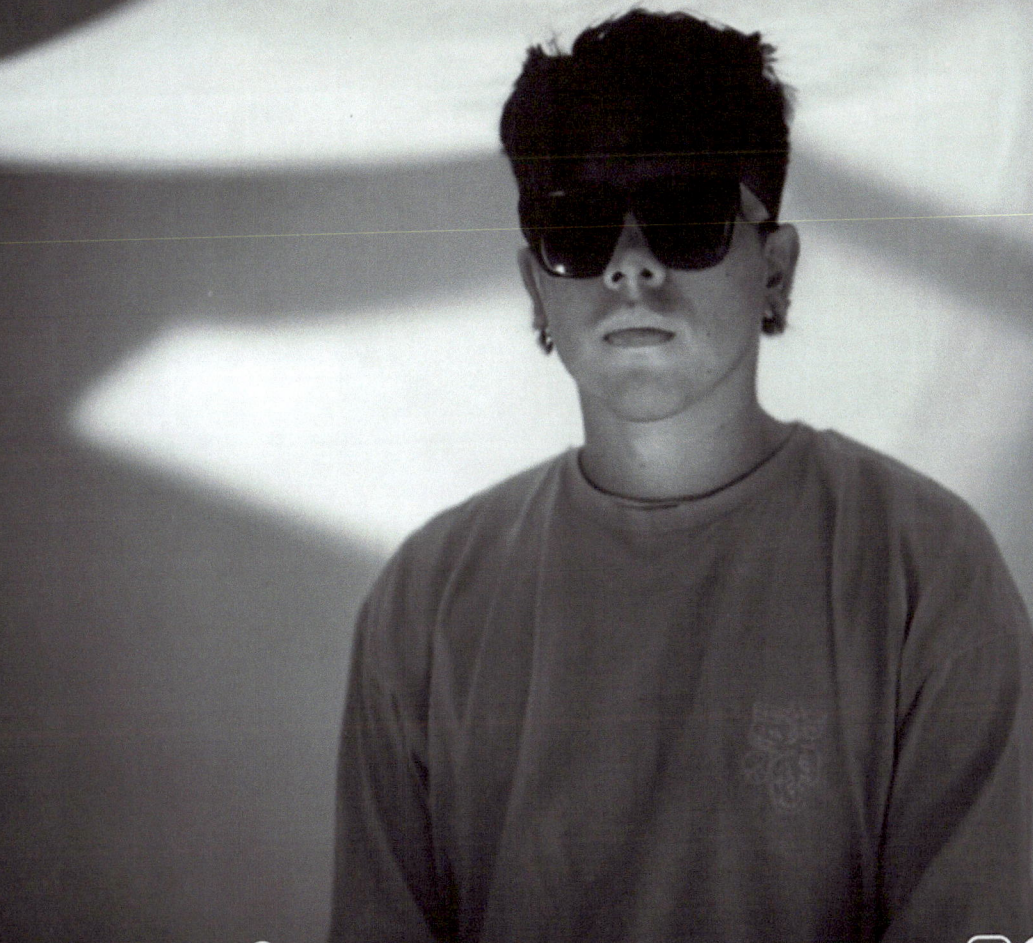

on proper aftercare to ensure the tattoo heals well without compromising any details. It's about finding that sweet spot where the tattoo looks stunning and remains vibrant over time.

My experience with DGN Tattoo Magazine and their contest was truly unforgettable. When I learned about the contest, I was excited to showcase my work and see how it would be received by the tattooing community. Participating in the contest gave me the opportunity to connect with fellow artists, share insights, and be a part of something larger within the industry.

Being recognized as one of the top 5 tattoo artists is an incredible honor. It's a validation of the passion and dedication I've poured into my craft. The acknowledgement from peers and professionals in the field is not only humbling but also motivating. This recognition fuels my desire to continuously improve, learn, and create meaningful art that resonates with people. The contest pushed me to refine my skills, step outside my comfort zone, and showcase my unique artistic style. Being part of this competition has not only expanded my horizons but also solidified my belief in the power of artistic expression through tattooing.

Tattoo stop: Inkfamous tattoo gallery - Bratislava / Eslovaquia
@snower_tattoo - Web: www.snowertattoo.com

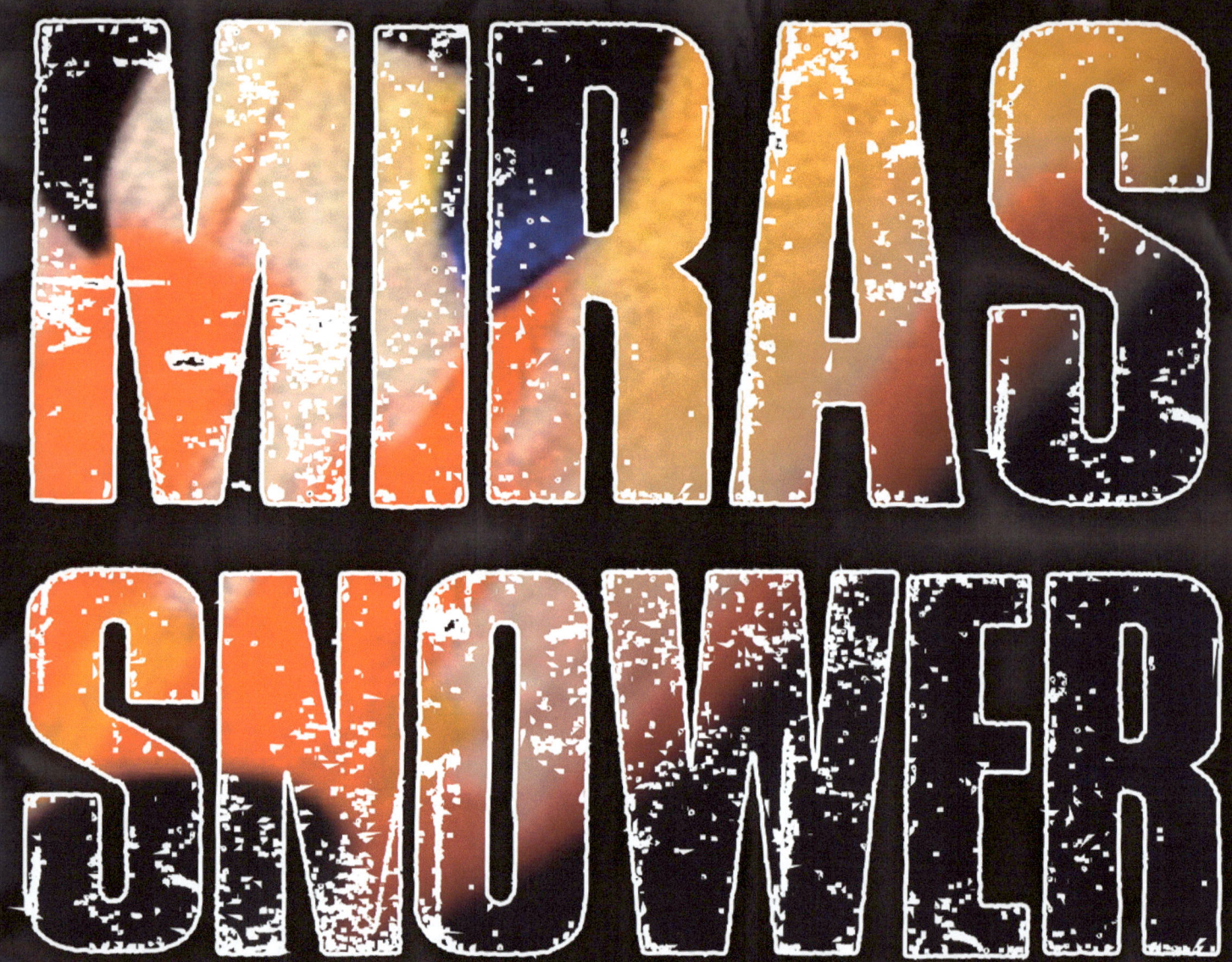

MIRAS SNOWER

Tattoo Artistry Beyond Boundaries

Known as "Snower," this tattoo artist has carved an exceptional artistic journey from a picturesque Czech village to his prominent position at the "Inkfamous" tattoo studio in Slovakia. His evolution in the world of tattooing is extraordinary, marked by his dedication to mastering diverse styles and his recent achievement as one of the top five finalists in a global tattoo competition, judged by renowned experts. Snower's story is a testament to the power of passion, talent, and the relentless pursuit of artistic excellence.

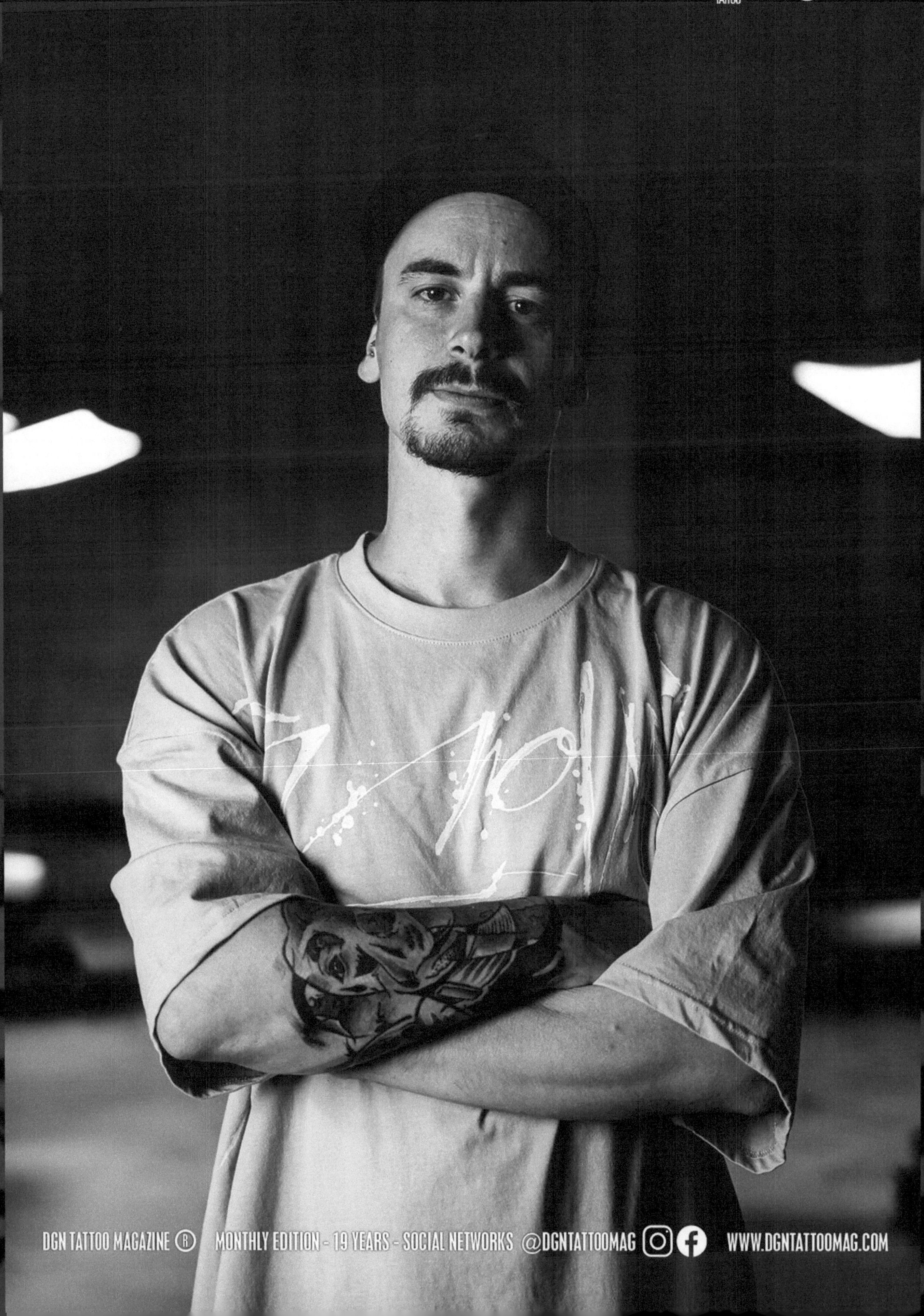

dgntattoomag 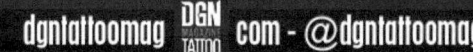 com - @dgntattoomag

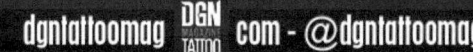

DGN TATTOO MAGAZINE ® MONTHLY EDITION - 19 YEARS - SOCIAL NETWORKS @DGNTATTOOMAG ⭕ f WWW.DGNTATTOOMAG.COM

At 33 years old, the internationally renowned tattoo artist, known as "Snower," has carved a path in the art world that transcends the ordinary. His story begins in 2014, in a picturesque village in the Czech Republic, where Snower took his first steps into the exciting world of body art. In those early days, he found a mentor in the oldest tattoo shop in the region, a mentor who imparted a vital philosophy: master every possible style. Though the direction of his art was initially unclear, this advice sowed the seeds of diverse and profound learning, ranging from creating mandalas to the elegance of calligraphy, the artistic representation of animals, and the complexity of portraits.

Snower fondly recalls those early years: "It was a period of discovery and constant learning. I learned to forge my own path in the art of tattooing, exploring every corner of the artistic spectrum."

After a couple of years, Snower took a bold leap by opening his own tattoo shop. It was then that he began experimenting with colors and delving into the intriguing world of watercolor style. This phase was marked by meticulous craftsmanship, as each design was painstakingly hand-drawn. This allowed him to immerse himself deeply in exploring colors, shapes, and proportions. Snower's passion for knowledge and artistic refinement grew insatiable.

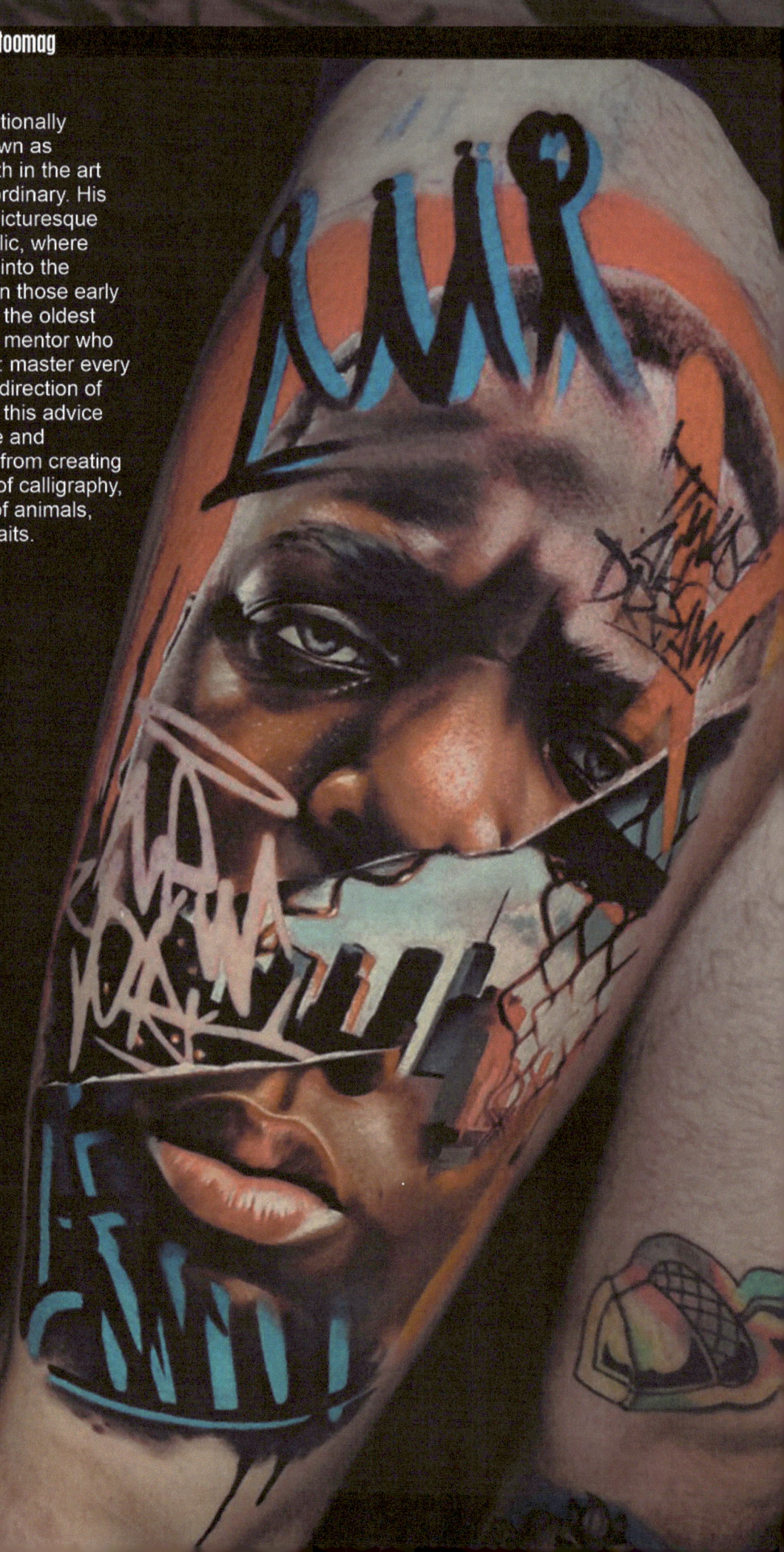

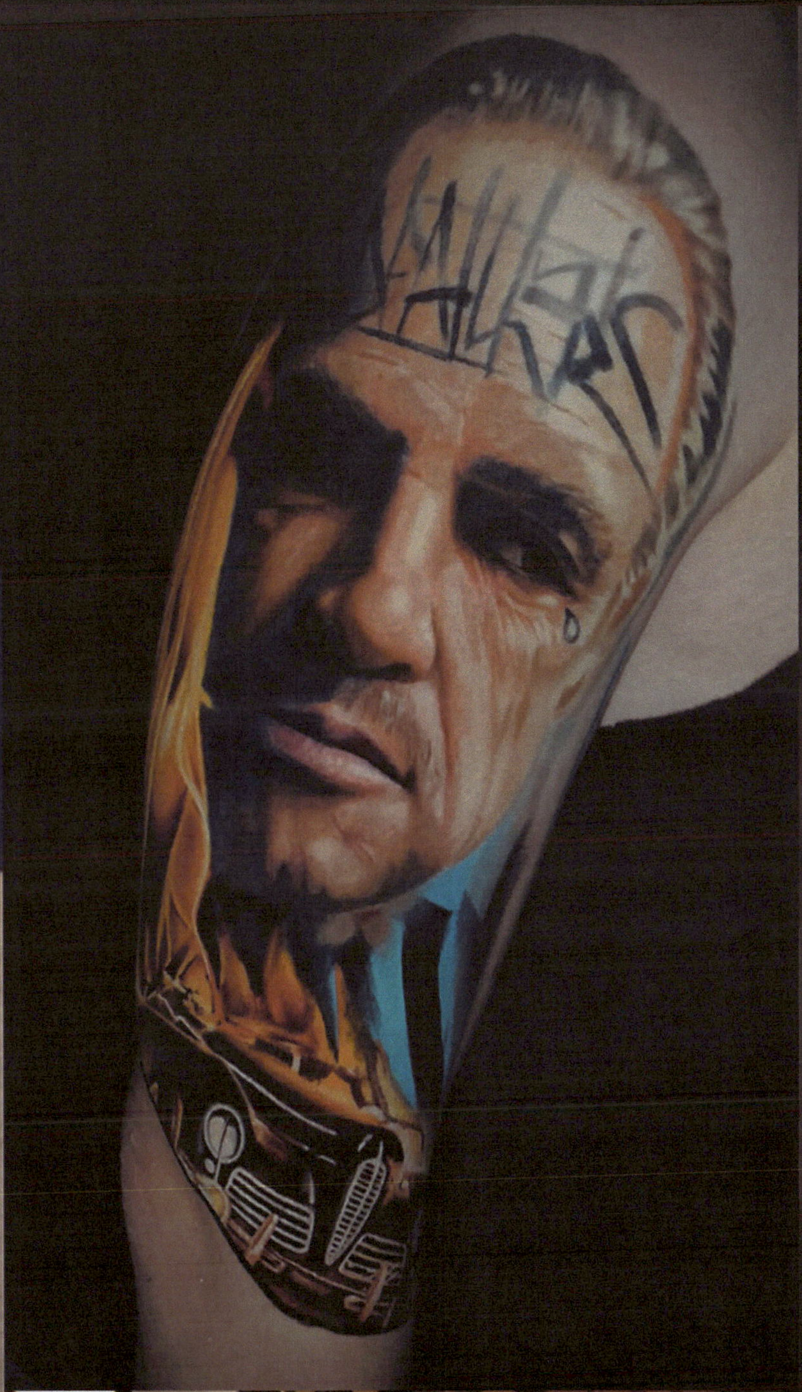

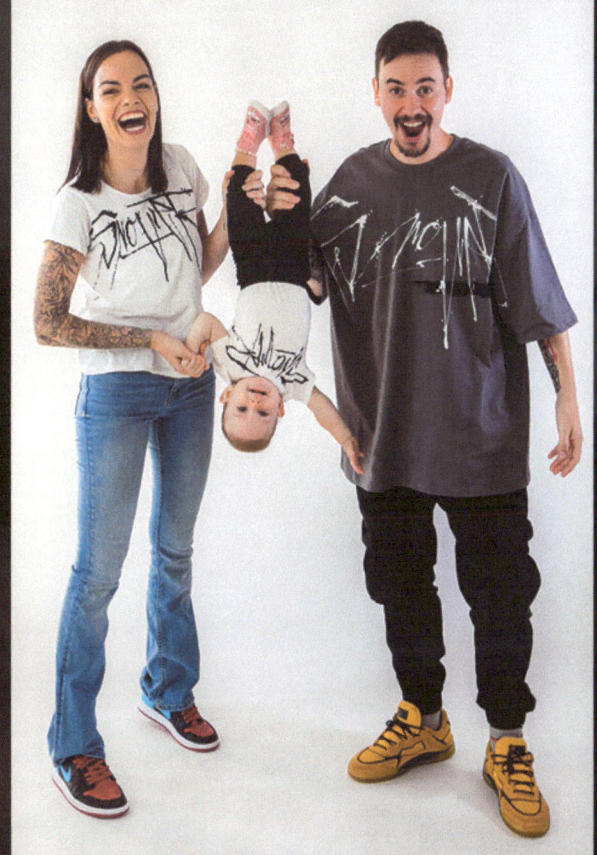

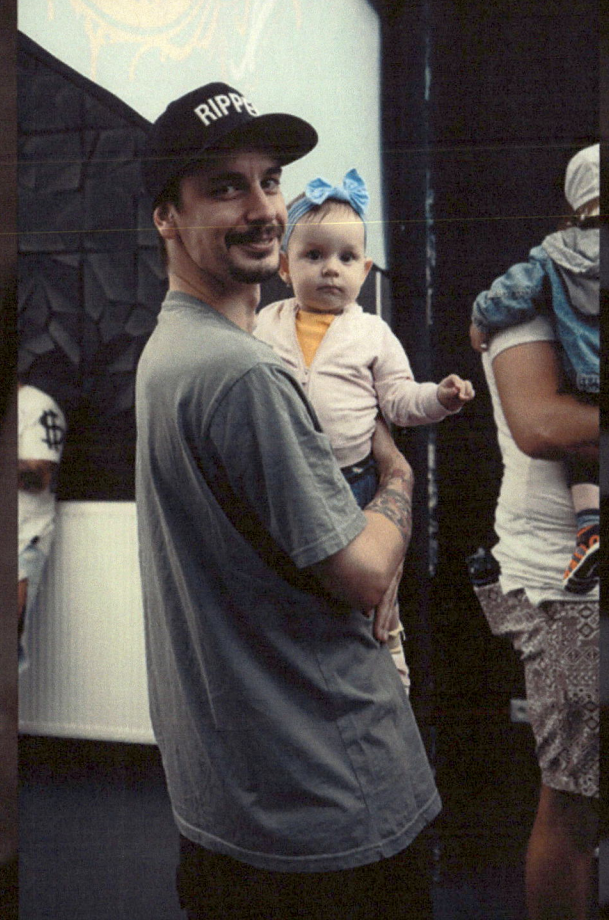

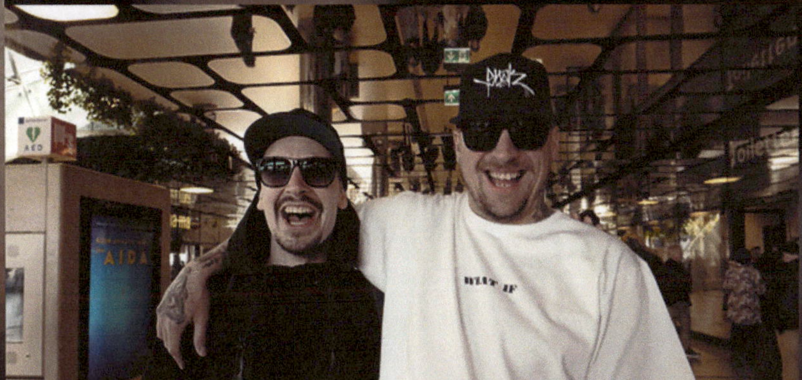

However, Snower was not destined to remain in his comfort zone. His thirst for knowledge led him to close his own shop and embark on a journey that took him to numerous places as a guest artist and assistant in tattoo seminars. It was at this point that he underwent a significant artistic transformation, shifting from the watercolor style to a more focused approach on stylized realism and realism with graphic elements and graffiti.

"The journey and exposure to different artistic approaches led me to evolve as a tattoo artist. I learned to appreciate diversity and embrace new challenges as opportunities for growth," Snower shares with a reflective smile.

Today, Snower is a prominent figure in the team of artists at the prestigious "Inkfamous" tattoo studio in Bratislava, Slovakia. There, he continues to perfect his art and keep his passion for tattooing alive. His commitment to artistic excellence leads him to closely follow the work of the best artists and stay updated on the latest trends and publications in tattoo culture.

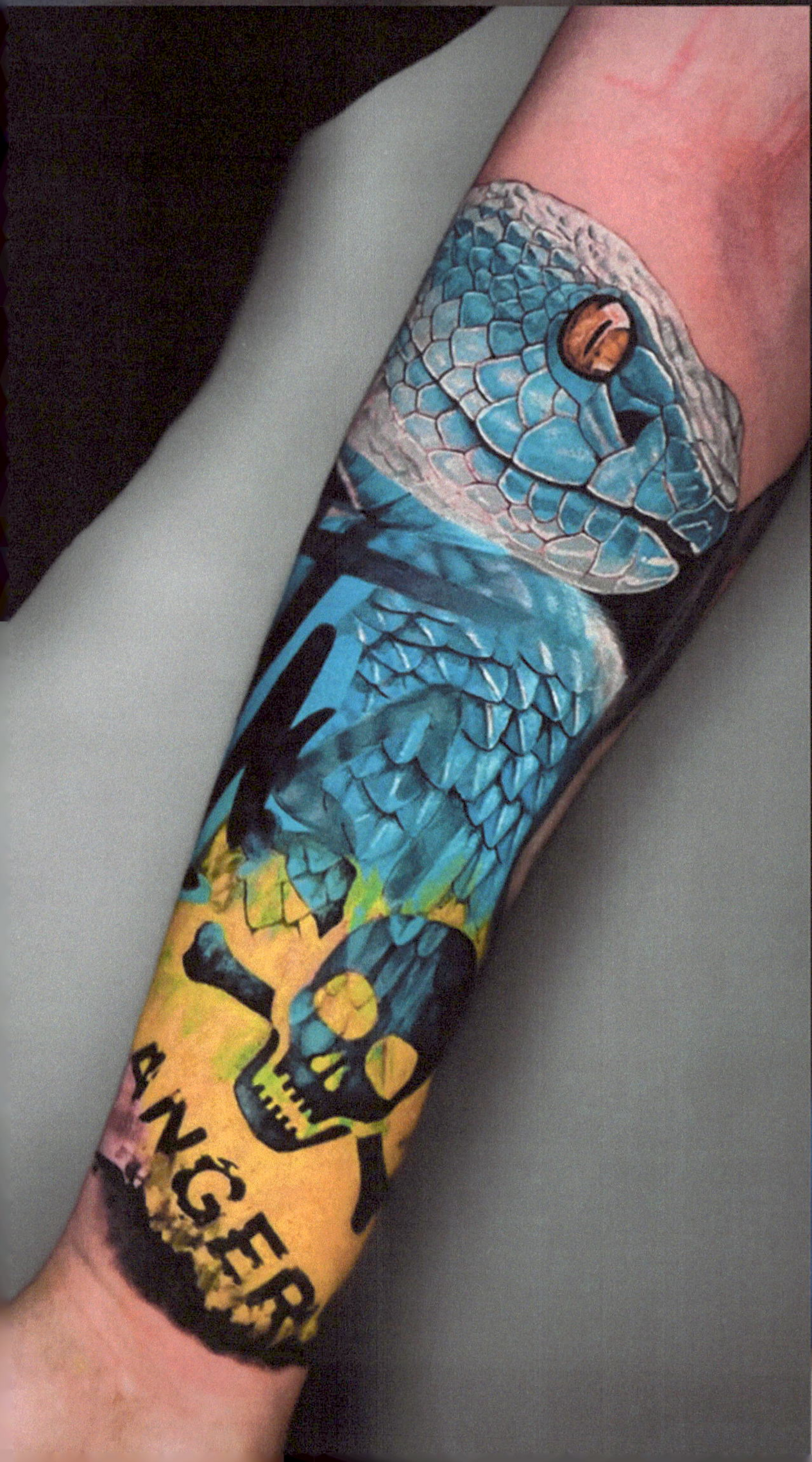

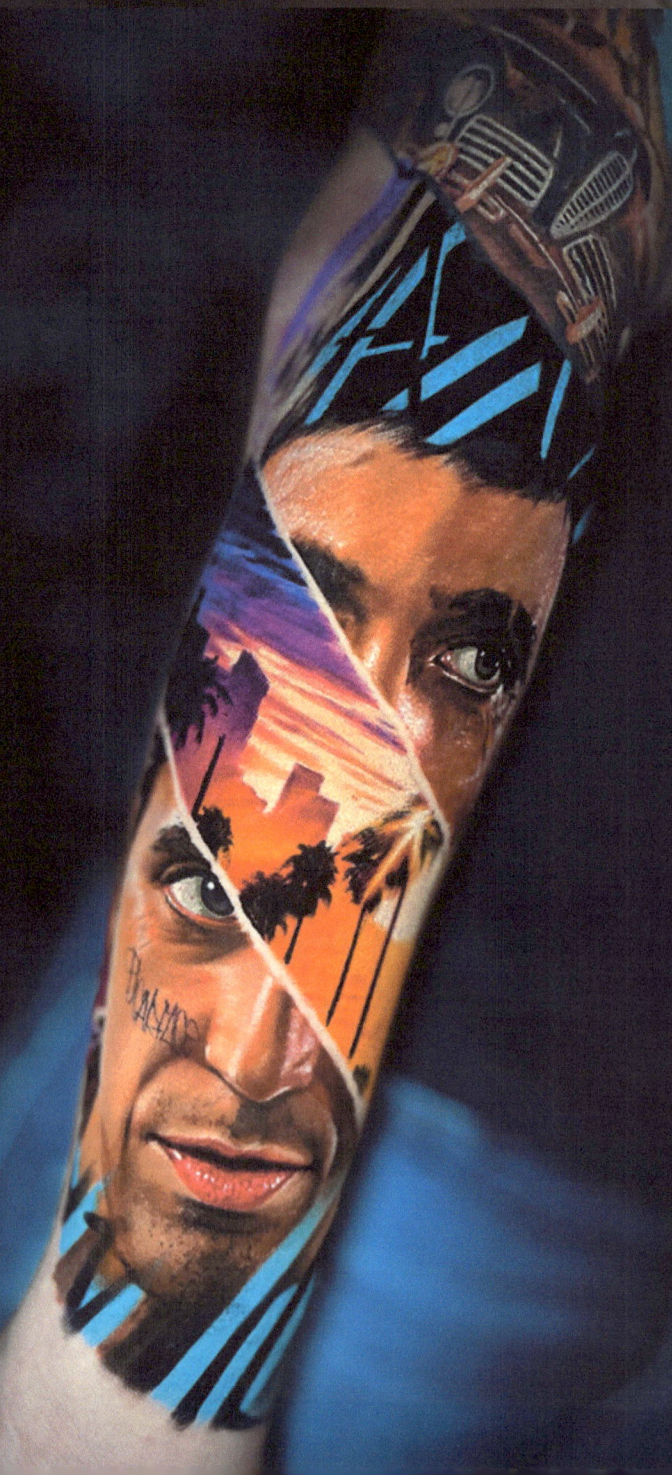

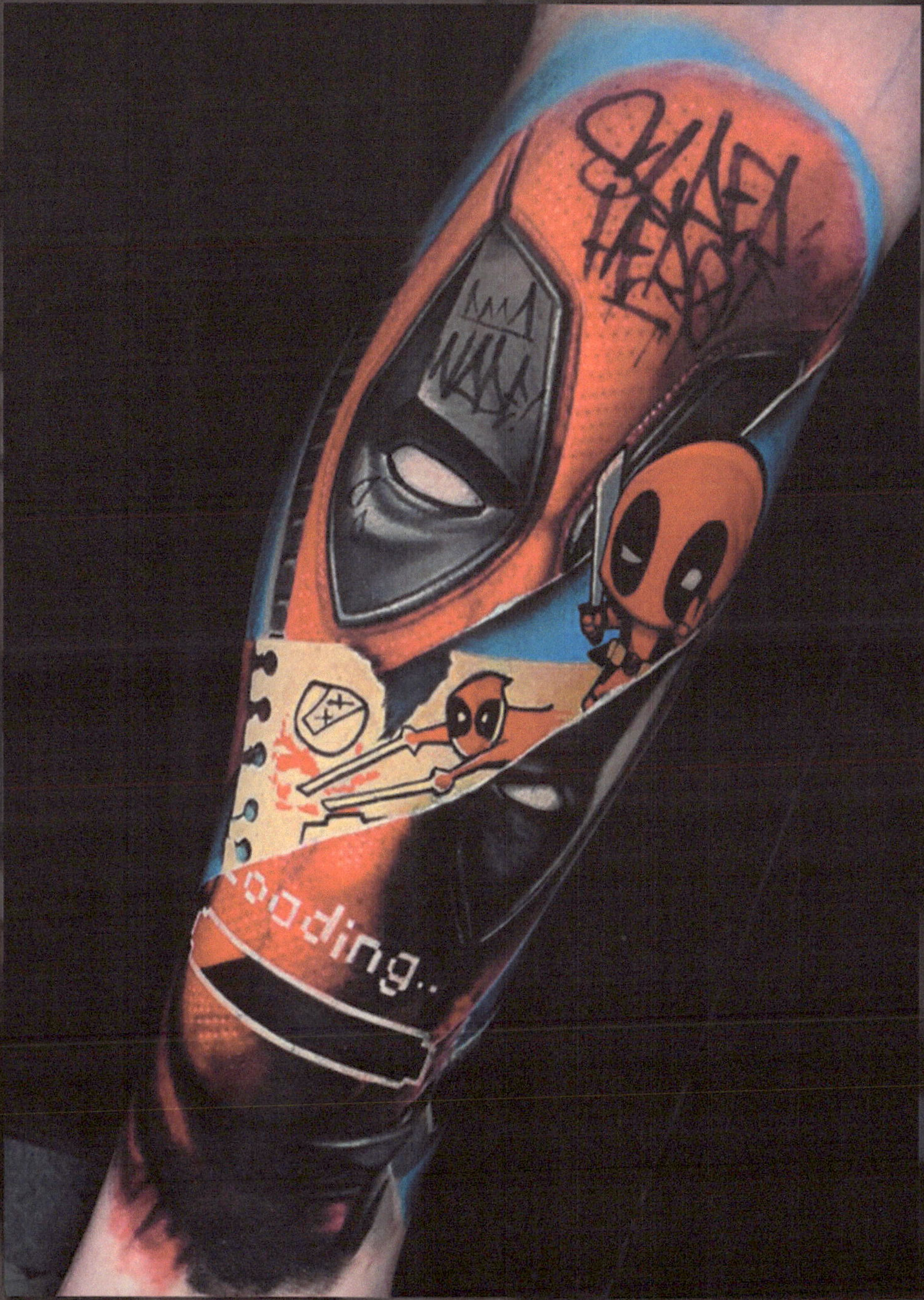

dgntattoomag **DGN** com - @dgntattoomag

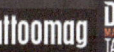

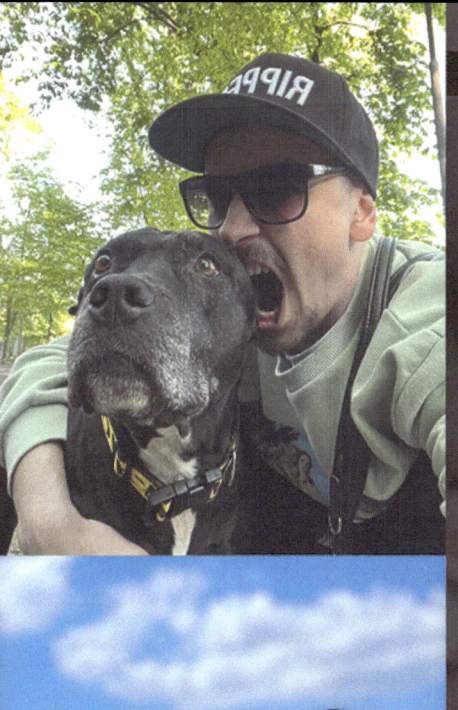

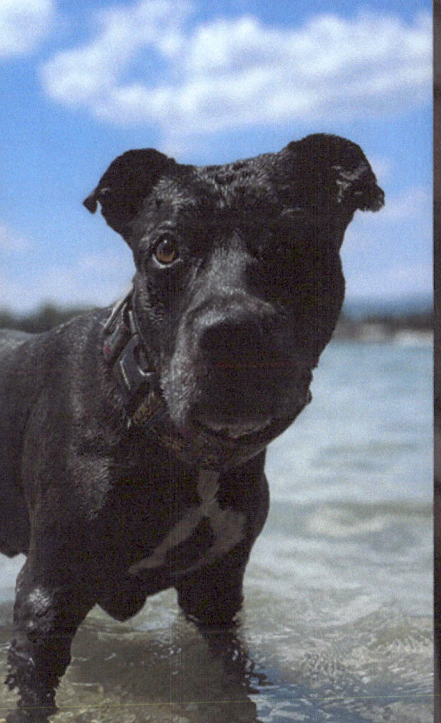

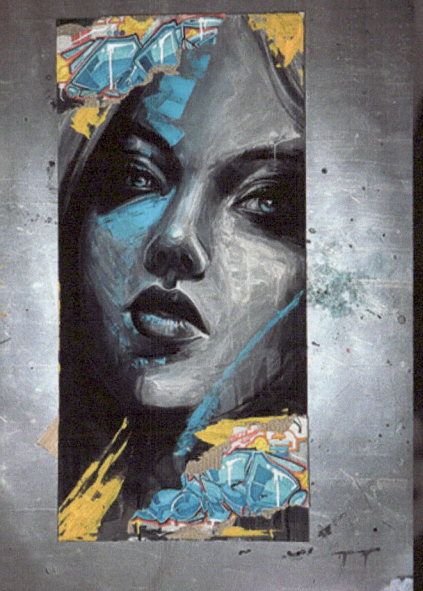

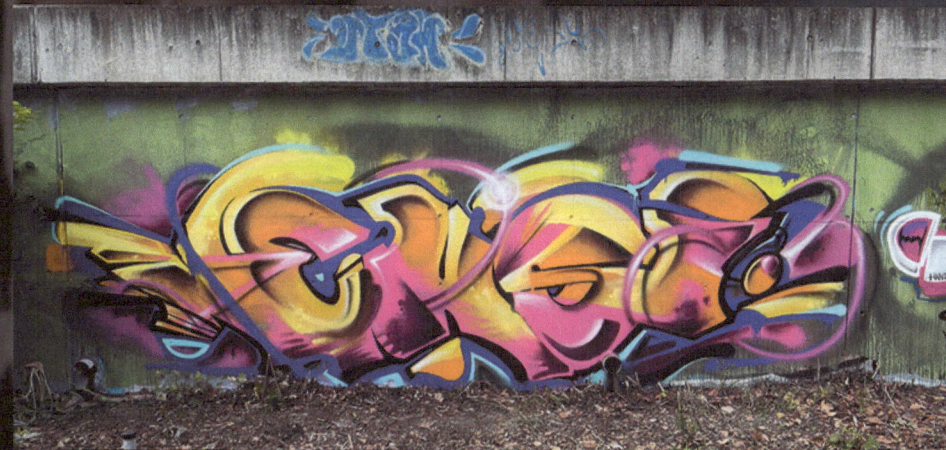

DGN TATTOO MAGAZINE ®   MONTHLY EDITION - 19 YEARS - SOCIAL NETWORKS @DGNTATTOOMAG WWW.DGNTATTOOMAG.COM

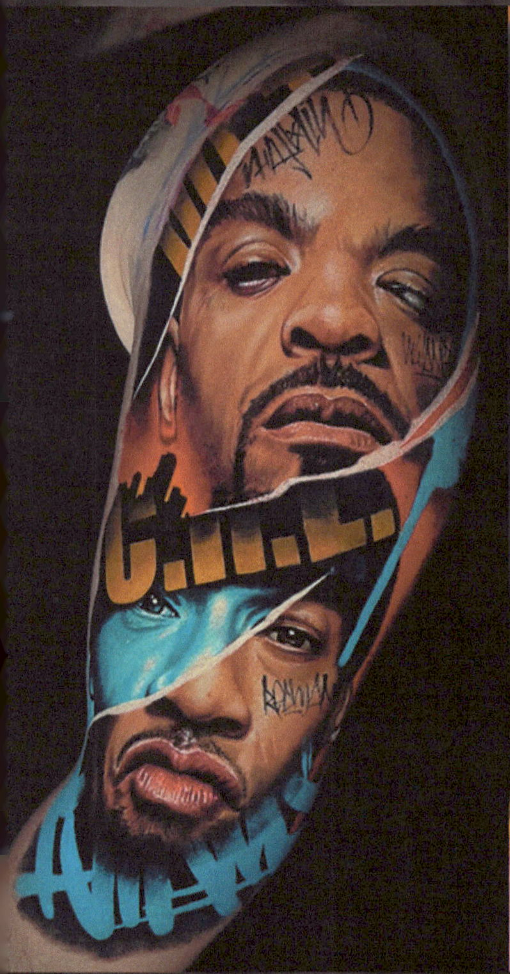

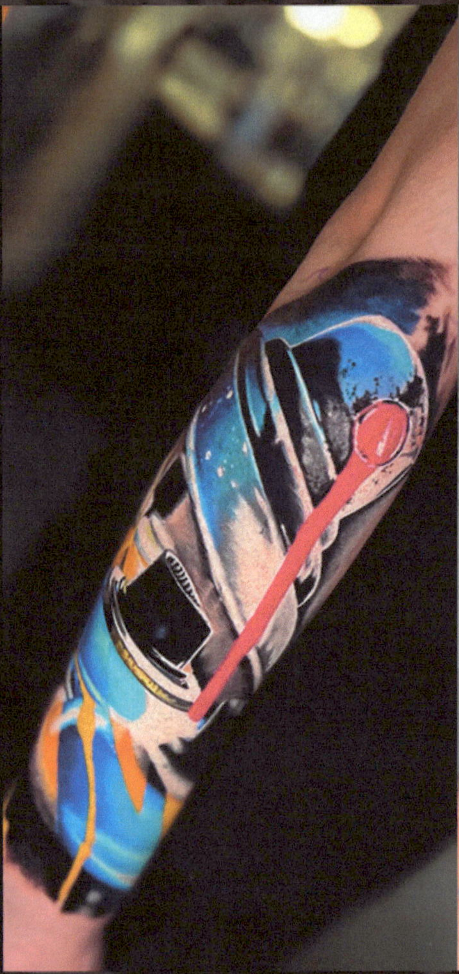

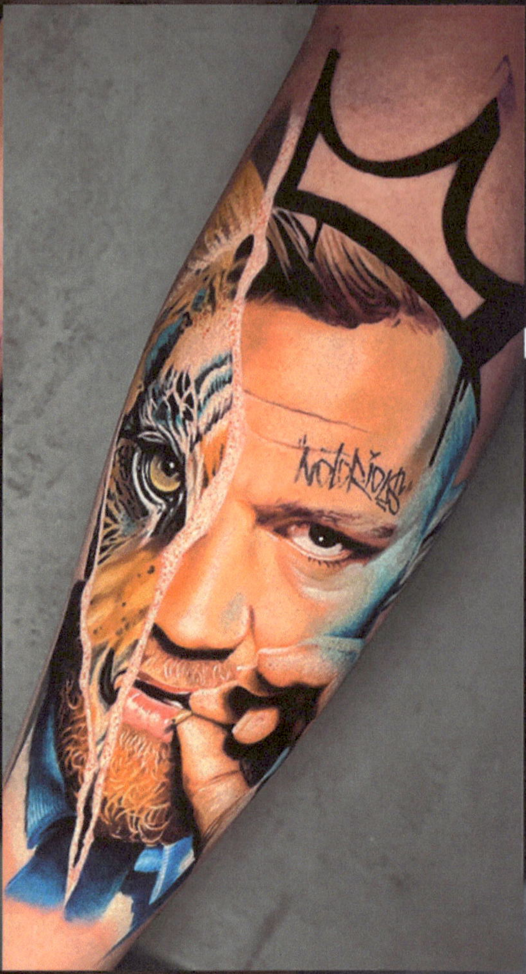

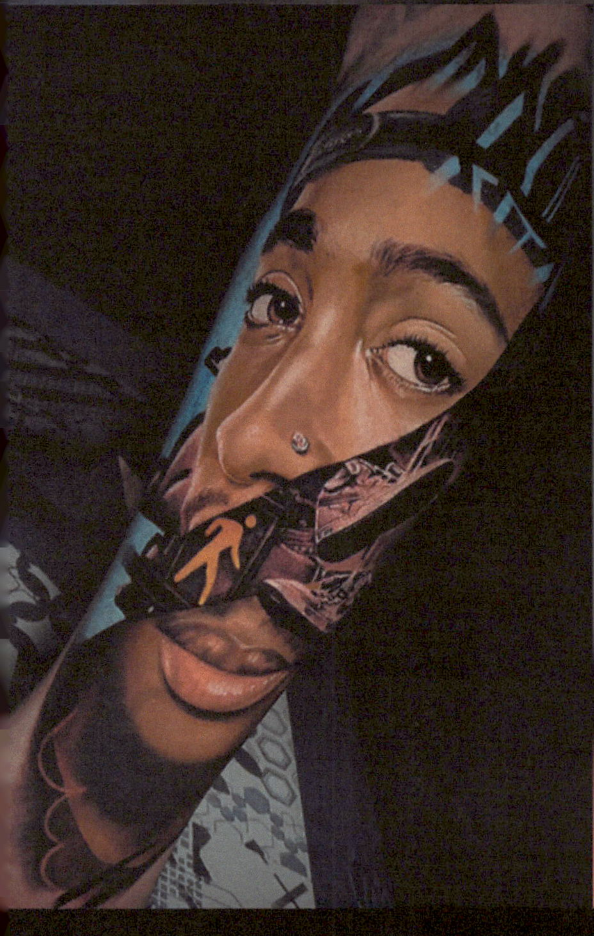

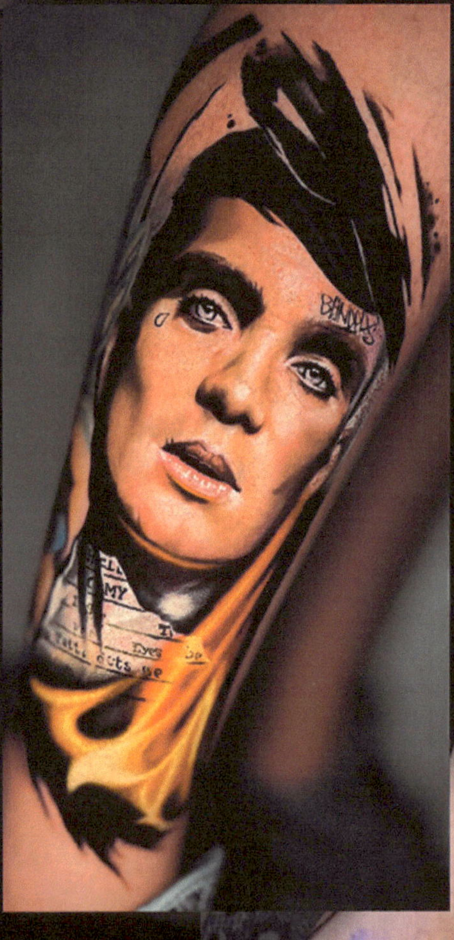

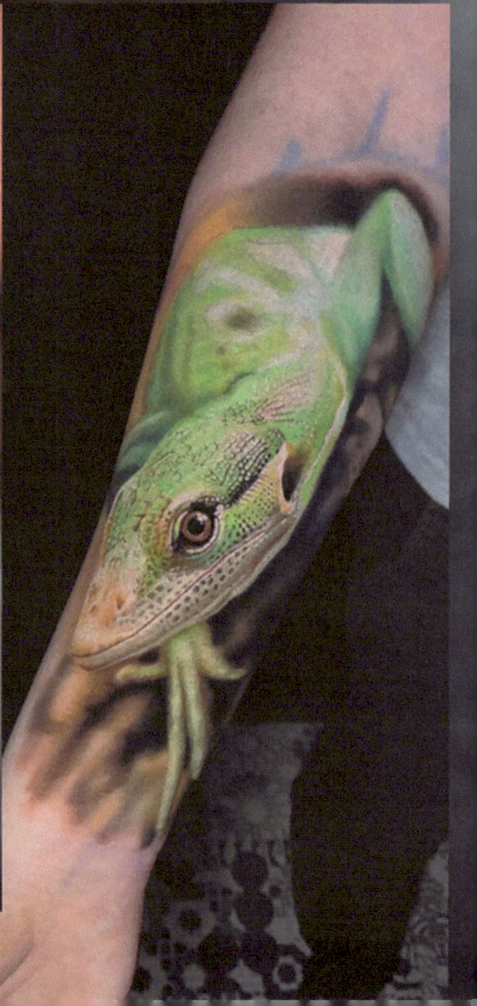

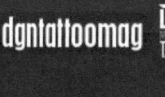
The pinnacle of his career came with the opportunity to participate in a global tattoo competition organized by one of the most respected magazines in the industry. The competition was fierce, and the jury included illustrious names like Myke Chambers, Dave Paulo, Valentina Riabova, Victor Portugal, Andrei Stepanov, and Haewall. Initially, Snower did not see himself as a standout competitor in such a prestigious event.

"Seeing those renowned artists on the jury was an overwhelming experience. I never imagined I could go this far," Snower humbly admits.

Nevertheless, Snower closely followed the competition's developments and was pleasantly surprised to discover the abundance of talented tattoo artists he had yet to hear about. The true surprise came when he learned that he had become one of the top five finalists, an achievement he considers one of the highlights of his career. As Snower points out, "Being among the top five tattoo artists worldwide is an honor and a testament to how perseverance and dedication can open surprising doors."

In summary, Snower's story is an inspiring testament to how passion, talent, and dedication can lead to extraordinary success in the world of tattoo artistry. His words reflect his journey of self-discovery and constant growth in an ever-evolving artistic world. His position among the top five tattoo artists globally, recognized by a prestigious jury, underscores his excellence and promises a bright future filled with achievements.

 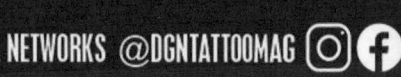

KULə

A GLOBAL GATHERING

18, 19, 20 & 21 JAN 2024
NESCO CENTER MUMBAI

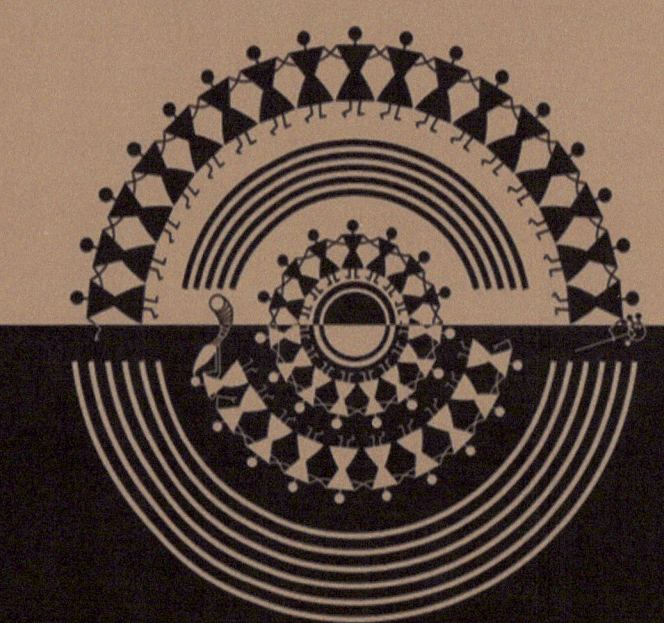

CO-EXISTING FOR A SHARED FUTURE

TATTOO - GRAFFITI - MUSIC
PIERCINGS - PERFORMING ARTS
STREET CULTURE

🌐 WWW.KULAWORLDWIDE.COM | 📷 KULAWORLDWIDE

www.ingramcontent.com/pod-product-compliance
Lightning Source LLC
Chambersburg PA
CBHW041511280526
45792CB00004B/1209